one more LAST CAST

ON THE ADDICTIVE NATURE OF FISHING

Dennis D. Dauble

Artwork by Ronald Reed

FishHead Press, Richland, Washington

Published by:
FishHead Press
3029 Sonoran Drive
Richland, WA 99354
www.dennisdauble.com

In cooperation with:
Keokee Co. Publishing, Inc.
405 Church Street
Sandpoint, ID 83864
(208) 263-3573
www.keokeebooks.com

ISBN 978-1537185309
Cover photo by Ronald Reed
Interior photos by author
Printed in the United State of America

. . . A PERFECT LAST CAST IS CATCHING A FISH AFTER
WHICH I WILL RETIRE FOR THE NIGHT.
—THOMAS MCGUANE

GO ON AHEAD AND TRY FOR HIM. HE'LL HIT A COUPLE
OF TIMES MORE, BUT YOU WON'T CATCH HIM.
- RICHARD BRAUTIGAN

TABLE OF CONTENTS

Acknowledgments v

Preface ix

Part 1. Home Waters 1

One More Last Cast 3

Sockeye Madness 9

Guinea Hen Steelhead 17

On Being Second-Rate 23

Cranky Motors 31

Daran's Rod 35

Six Colors 41

Shuffleboard Excursion 47

Getting Your Due 55

Addiction 61

Part 2. Far-Flung Adventures 71

Hurricanes, Dorado, and Bar Soap 73

She-Boy-Gun 85

Eight Seconds 91

109 Steps 95

Redtails and High Tide 105

Part 3. Human Nature 113

Coulee Town 115

Two Pillow Sleepers 121

A Fish for Mom 127

Leaky Waders 133

Spam Picnic 137

Trails of Evidence 141

Bucks and Does 145

Scent and Sensibility 149

Losing it 153

Everything Counts for Something 161

ACKNOWLEDGMENTS

MAYBE IT'S MY IMAGINATION, but some folks snap to attention when I quit casting and sit down to make notes in my pocket journal. "You're not going to use that against me, are you?" they ask. "Just making notes," I reply. "It's difficult to remember details." (Not to mention incriminating behavior and interesting conversation I couldn't otherwise reconstruct.)

The nature of responses can be broad, ranging from, "Print whatever you want, but you had better delete any and all reference to my location, method, and behavior," to "Awesome! Do I get a free copy of your book when it comes out?" As a consequence of this feedback, certain character names and locales have been altered to preserve their anonymity.

The simple truth is, these stories would not have happened if not for friends and family who tolerated my companionship on the water. For that I am grateful. In particular, I appreciate the following individuals who provided constructive comment on stories: Dale Becker, Ken Gano, Bobby Loomis, Geoff McMichael, Bob Mueller, Ted Poston, Ronald Reed, and Brett Tiller. And special thanks to Leroy, who started it all. Finally, I thank my best friend and wife, Nancy, for her insight and support for my writing.

The look and feel of this book benefited from interior illustrations fashioned by the creative hand of Ronald Reed. Cover design and layout was by Laura Wahl.

Some parts of the following stories first appeared in these other publications: "Two Pillow Sleepers," "Trails of Evidence," and "Eight Seconds" in *Northwest Sportsman*; "Bucks and Does" in the *Tri-City Herald*; "Guinea Hen Steelhead" in *Washington-Oregon Game & Fish*; "109 Steps" in *Alaska Sporting Journal*.

MY CONCERN, IN THIS BOOK, IS NOT WITH MY OWN
WANDERINGS, OR STATE OF MINDS.

—GONTRAN DE PONCINS

PREFACE

THESE STORIES did not come to me like musings to a poet. They mostly wrote themselves. That's the beauty of true-life adventure. It's a rare day on the water when something does not come up worth mentioning, whether success, anecdote, or foible. You don't have to search for material like a journalist on assignment. Indeed, many stories came about when I merely showed up and paid attention. Others were the result of reinforcement. When the same thing happens over and over again, it's time to take notice. Then there are stories that remind us that certain opinions are better kept to oneself, although admittedly that's something I've never been good at.

If you are like me, fishing creeps into your thoughts, conversation, and dreams. While watching, listening to, and reflecting on the idiosyncratic behavior of others was crucial to the development of this collection, I prefer to think that doing so was not an obsession. *Obsession* would be too strong a word. Nonetheless, you could say I have been known to dwell on the transcendental connection between everyday activities and angling to the point of introspection. Like you might examine your belly button to gain insight on the origin of the species, gaze at the heavens as if black holes truly influence your universe, or when my 22-year-old cockatiel, Spike, examines the tiny silver bell that dangles next to his perch and wonders, "Is this a toy or my girlfriend?"

Not to dwell on quirky behavior, but there is little doubt that fishing fulfills a deep emotional need for many of us. Indeed, for some anglers, this need can lead to addiction. Consider that a non-addict has the willpower to state "one more last cast" and quit. It matters not if they experience a cerebral moment, a missed strike, or view a series of aggressive rises. Not so for the addict. The addict requires little if any excuse to continue past the designated quitting time and will do so until you wrench the rod out of their cold, stiff fingers. It seems the privilege to fish for as long as you want is a constitutional right in some circles.

Regardless of shortcoming in syntax, interpretation of fact and sensitivity (all of which can be ascribed to me), my hope is that each story reads as honest as lyrics from a John Prine album, seems as familiar as a Tom Petty ballad, yet some passages echo with an occasional Jimi Hendrix guitar lick (to keep you alert). Keeping with a musical analogy, I tried not to hit the same wrong note twice.

This book is for my big brother Daran, a master at revealing his innermost thoughts for the sake of story. I helped spread his ashes on a sandy beach in Oregon where we once casted for surfperch until Mom called us in for supper. He was generous and patient, but a lousy fisherman. I think about him often.

DDD, June 2016

Grain elevator above the Touchet River near Prescott, Washington.

PART I. HOME WATERS

ONCE YOU GET THE HABIT OF LOOKING FOR GOOD
PLACES FOR FISH TO BE, YOU NEVER LOSE IT.
—IAN FRAZIER

ONE MORE LAST CAST

THE TOPIC OF WHAT CONSTITUTES quitting time with your rod and reel came up during and after a work get-together with friends at the local White Bluffs Brewery. After work for them, that is. In my retiree world, every day is a holiday.

I remember how my first beer was chugged from the side of the road when I was 15 years old. Back then it was all about "the water." Nowadays it's about malts and hops. IPAs, stouts, and Hefeweizens were not ordered from patrons sitting on bar stools when I grew up in the farmlands of northeastern Oregon. Except for the occasional malt liquor, which was considered a gateway brew to "hard stuff," everyone drank lager. If you wanted variety, you chose a different shape or color of bottle.

But libation has come a long way. The drinking public demands it. A single premium beer costs as much as what you used to spend for a six-pack and comes rated according to alcohol by volume (ABV) and International Bitterness Unit (IBU). I understand ABV or the alcohol content part, but admit to confusion over the meaning of parts per million of isohumulone. Another difference is that taverns used to mean old guys sipping from a brown bottle, cigarette smoke wafting in air, and Patsy Cline on the jukebox. Nowadays, drinking establishments are more apt to showcase mixed genders from age 21 to 81, tap brews in a pint glass, and the sound of laughter.

These thoughts took shape as I nursed a 12-ounce, consumer-sized glass of Red Alt (6.0 ABV; 32 IBUs). Meanwhile, my hophead friends were halfway through their second pint of Bluff Diver IPA (7.7 ABV; 96 IBUs). After sitting on a shiny high-back stainless steel chair for an hour, I couldn't help but do the math. Clearly, they held advantage over me.

About then, GM initiated conversation with a recap of his last fishing trip. "I told Scott we had time for one last cast, but when I looked over and saw he wasn't paying attention, I tossed out again," he said. "And again," demonstrating a series of underarm casts, while feigning a guilty look at Scott.

Scott gazed into space and ignored GM's animated version of casting as if to mimic his lack of interest in the previous scenario.

"I usually quit steelhead fishing after I break off a rig," I said. "My last cast is often an impossible presentation: over a logjam, into a pile of boulders, through an overhanging limb. A "Hail Mary" cast. The kind you make when you've given up on catching a fish but don't feel like going home."

There was no way to predict how long I could hold the floor, so I continued. "Although, I've been known to tie on a new rig on the hike back to my truck and revisit a hole that didn't yield a fish earlier in the day. One more last cast, so to speak. When I actually quit, however, depends on how long it's past the time I told Nancy I would be home."

After a long pull on his foaming brew, Kyle spoke up. "I prefer to quit on a fish," he declared, in a tone that implied, Why consider anything else?

"Nice idea, but not always possible," I argued. "Sometimes that last fish never happens. I could see your plan working out if the goal was to catch your limit, though. For instance, when I go fish for trout, I hang onto that next-to-last keeper for a long time before I quit, and practice catch-and-release to stretch out the day.

"You could quit when it gets dark," Scott said, steering his way in the direction of the restroom. "Excuse me, but I've got to see a man about a horse."

"Darkness works, also," Kyle replied. "It's easier to quit when you can't see where you're casting or can't tie a knot. Of course, there's always a head lamp"

"Or a full moon," I said, remembering when John and I had packed our float tubes to fish Mary Lake near Mattawa. Trout didn't start biting until after the sun dropped low over the sage. We told our wives we would be home by dark, but action got hot when the full moon rose over Sentinel Gap. There's something about a 3-pound rainbow taking you down to the backing that keeps you fishing well past quitting time.

"Bob gives a time to quit when we're out in his boat, but we usually fish longer," I said.

"That never works for me, either," GM laughed.

"Bringing up time does provide an entry for the topic of when to quit, however," Kyle said, adding an intellectual twist to a topic at risk of turning as flat as the last swallow of lukewarm beer in my glass.

"Like an ice-breaker."

"As a means to initiate further discussion, because sooner or later, you have to reel in for the day."

Bob merely nodded his head in a midwestern manner that suggested general agreement. Either that or the gesture was the side effect of his state of inebriation.

"Not to stretch things out," I said, "but here's another example. Leroy and I were fishing for yellow perch at Cargill Pond. We casted small jigs tipped with a piece of night crawler under a slip bobber. Six keeper-size perch were flopping in the bottom of my drink cooler, the bare minimum for a Saturday night fish fry. In contrast, Leroy was letting his 7-inchers go because he didn't want to go to the trouble of filleting them. When the after-church crowd showed up, he asked if I was ready to quit. I suggested we fish until we lost the bait on our hooks, and save the rest of my worms for another day. That's when Leroy baited up for the last time, and that's when he saw part of a night crawler laying on the ground by our Styrofoam bait container. 'Looks like we have two more baits,' he said. 'One more last cast for you and one more for me.'"

That's tavern talk for you. What it proves is that some folks are so focused on catching fish, you have to tear the rod out of their hands before they will quit. Consider my bass fishing buddy Wayne. If fishing is good, he doesn't stop until it's pitch-black out. If fishing is poor, he has to keep fishing until he figures out why.

The affliction is not limited to gear fishermen. Fly casters are just as bad. I remember watching my friend Ken work slowly down the Ringold shoreline one frosty-cold winter morning. I huddled in my truck after getting low-holed by two spin fishermen. There was a skim of ice along the shoreline, and a north wind ruffled the surface of the river. A hot bowl of chili sounded good, but the nearest one was 40 miles away. I couldn't help think that when your fingers are frozen, your fly ain't attracting, and the odds of catching a steelhead are slim to none, you might as well cut your losses and quit for the day.

Meanwhile, Ken swung his Purple Marabou across the gentle current as if he had all the time in the world. That is, until he wrapped his sink tip around a submerged boulder. After several minutes of trying to finesse the hook loose, he was forced to break it off. However, rather than wade back to shore to recoup, he stood in silent repose, as if doing so would reincarnate his lost tippet and fly. I rolled the truck window down when he looked in my direction and yelled, "That sucks!"

"Oh well, I was ready to quit," he replied, although something about his body language suggested otherwise.

The moral is that over-the-hill quarterbacks aren't the only ones who don't know when to quit. Gamblers go to the well for one last hand of poker, dopers roll another number for the road, and dedicated anglers strive for one more last cast.

one more LAST CAST

SOCKEYE MADNESS

"REMINDS ME OF FISH BAIT," I said when wife Nancy served up the entrée-sized portion of shrimp salad.

"What are you talking about?" she replied haughtily.

"Leroy and I tipped our hooks with shrimp when we fished for sockeye last week. The only difference between our bait and this salad is red krill."

Blame my obsession with sockeye on that red, white, and blue ball cap, the one with a distinctive fish skeleton logo. That's what caught my attention. That eye-catching hat and a card that read, "This Certificate is good for one angler to fish for a day with Mack's Lure Company President Bob Schmidt or National Sales Director Bob Loomis on a Northwest waterway to be determined. Estimated value $300."

You might say I was hooked. I was at a writer's conference, had $20 worth of raffle tickets in my hand and was tired of looking for a place to put them. You got it. All 40 tickets worth 50 cents each went into a half-gallon coffee can through a slit in the plastic lid. You might call it stuffing the ballot box. I call it power shopping. The result was, I won the guided trip.

Let me start by explaining that guided fishing trips are not my forte. There's something wrong about having someone bait your lure, set the hook, and pass you the rod. It's too much like being spoon-fed. I'd rather feed myself and dribble on my chin. But this trip might be different, I told myself. Plus, I would be going with developers of the world-famous Smile Blade!

After a series of e-mail exchanges with Bobby Loomis, I settled on a trip to Lake Wenatchee for sockeye salmon. Meanwhile, I didn't know if I would be sleeping in my truck, a no-tell motel, or at Bobby's house. Due to a lapse in communication, I woke up the day before the trip wondering if it was going to happen. What transpired was an e-mail to Leroy while I waited for a phone call from Bobby to resolve my angst.

My perfect guided fishing trip for sockeye would start off with a wakeup call from a soft-voiced woman, followed by a gentle pat on the shoulder. Next on my list would be a continental breakfast consisting of a tall glass of OJ, a warm pastry, and a cup of strong coffee. After a short drive to the fishing locale, we would stop to accommodate my GI tract. Once on the water, and following a brief instruction on the target fishery, I would hold my own rod, set my own hook, and fight my own fish. (Or lose my own fish, if that's the way it went down.)

After catching and releasing all the fish I wanted, we would barbecue hamburgers on the back of the boat and wash them down with premium beer. The guide would fillet my catch and put it on ice while his college-age daughter (blonde, ponytail, fit) would massage my aching back and shoulders to ease them from all the reeling and jerking.

Despite my apprehension, things turned out better than imagined. I was treated to dinner and drink at a local brewpub with Bobby and his lovely wife, and afterwards the adoring company of two crazy Boston terriers and an out-of-control Jack Russell. I slept soundly in a comfortable bed with clean sheets and pillow of choice. Wake-up service included Folgers' best, powdered jelly donuts and a fresh peach, served during a chauffeured drive to the boat launch. Expert guide service, provided by Bobby and his friend Richy, resulted in a boat limit of bronze-backed sockeye up to seven pounds. More importantly, they let me hold my rod, crank the downrigger, reel in my fish, and net theirs! The day was topped off with a box lunch that consisted of chips, leftover pizza, and smoked salmon, washed down with a 24-ounce Heineken.

Flash-forward three years later, this time for sockeye off the mouth of the Okanogan River. Taking what I learned on that inaugural trip to Lake Wenatchee and several positive experiences in the Hanford Reach, I now fancied myself a sockeye angler. To ready for the Okanogan trip, I studied an informative YouTube video that showed my former companions, Bobby and Richy, doing what they do best. It took all 9 minutes and 25 seconds for me to figure out where to attach my lead weight relative to the Double D dodger.

It had been some time since Leroy and I had tested each other's patience, but we weren't about to forego tradition and miss our annual summer outing to Brewster. What made the trip special was spending a night on the water instead of fighting the 2:00-a.m. crowd at the launch. Finding an open date on our calendars proved a challenge. Both spouses had medical issues, and playing the role of nursemaid had clipped our wings. The weather was another consideration. We arrived after a major thunderstorm one year to find sockeye halfway to Canada, and didn't wish for that to happen again.

But this year was different. Sunny skies and triple-digit temperatures kept thousands of sockeye stacked up in the cool waters of the Columbia off the mouth of the Okanogan River. Maybe we should have known better, but it was a surprise to find the riverside park in Brewster swarming with RVs, boat trailers, and campers on a weekday afternoon. It was obvious that many anglers were camped for the season. The only thing missing from the frenetic scene was cotton candy and caged exotic animals.

We also didn't expect to find more than 30 boats on the water when the average afternoon count the year before was half a dozen. Nonetheless, we took advantage of two-pole endorsements to gear up four outfits: two downriggers and two "bonus" rods with 5-ounce lead droppers. Our rust showed. I tangled my Double D dodger and Smile Blade rig on a downrigger cable while making a sharp turn. The first net job backfired when Leroy's lead ball dropper got hung up in the net mesh. We lost another sockeye when it wrapped around another boat's prop.

The boat count approached fifty, with a strong bite in effect, until the afternoon sun dropped below the west canyon wall. Leroy and I had managed to land four sockeye (what we deemed a "minimum acceptable unit"), but our batting average was poor due to all the screw-ups. Certainly more screw-ups than you might expect from two seasoned salmon anglers.

"Tomorrow will be better," I said to Leroy as we prepared for a night on the boat. Luminescent stars filled the sky on a new-moon night as a light chop lulled us to sleep. I napped soundly until an hour before dawn, when the first boat arrived on the water. There were 20 boats in constant motion when we rolled up our sleeping bags, and Leroy counted 40 when we fired up the kicker at 5:00 a.m. Luckily, we had learned a few things the afternoon before. Got the kinks out, so to speak. But fishing was more challenging given the large number of boats that competed for troll lines.

Everywhere we looked, there were boats. There were boats that trailed behind you, boats that cut across your bow and boats that pointed at you. "Crazy, huh?" I said to a nearby angler who cut off my troll path. By mid-morning, more than 150 boats were within view, ranging from car-toppers to party boats and everything in between, trolling 1 to 2 miles per hour in a slow-paced melee. *This was not fishing,* I thought. *It was cutthroat competition.* Given the situation, Leroy focused on watching the rods while I stayed vigilant at the tiller. The scene reminded of a LA traffic jam. "Can't take my eyes off the road," I said.

"Better you than me," Leroy replied. "All I know is if I was driving the boat, we'd be fishing somewhere else."

"And not catching fish," I said. "We've got no choice but to mix it up if we want to put sockeye in the box."

The morning began with me knocking Leroy's first sockeye off at the net, but I netted the next two that swam towards the boat obediently. Shutting the kicker motor off to fight a fish was not an option. Given the general melee before us, our troll speed and direction had to be controlled at all times. Catching a sockeye was not about playing them out. It was about getting them into the boat as quickly as possible without confrontation.

When Leroy hooked a fish, I managed the trolling motor until he brought the fish close, ignoring his: "Get the net!" shouts for as long as possible. One quick swipe, fish and net tossed on the bottom of the boat, and I resumed my place at the tiller. Thank goodness for a kicker motor that ran smooth and steady at low speed.

Things got tense after I netted Leroy's third mint-bright sockeye of the morning and my rod jack-hammered to the tune of another. I reeled the fish to the back of the boat and waited for Leroy to give me a hand. "Need a net here!" I yelled.

"My lead ball is tangled in the net!" he yelled back.

"Get it figured out quick and net this fish!"

"I need a knife to cut it out!"

With one hand on the tiller and another on my rod, I didn't have the option of handing him my pocketknife. And we weren't good enough friends to let him reach in my front pocket and get it for himself. "Where's your knife?" I yelled. "This fish is ready to come in!"

"I can't find it!" he said, on his knees now, with his back to me, messing with the tangled rig.

That's when I recalled the part of the YouTube video where Bobby Loomis led a small sockeye to the back of the boat, rod tip pointed down to prevent it from splashing wildly at the surface, no net in sight. With one quick motion, Bobby pulled the sockeye out of the water and into the bottom of the boat, a technique known as "railing."

"There's a trick to it," he later explained. "It mostly has to do with keeping the fish moving in your direction."

With that sage advice still in the future, I took one last look at Leroy's bent-over figure and reeled the wildly thrashing sockeye up to my dodger. Doing my best imitation of Bobby's railing technique, I jerked the 4-pounder out of the water and dragged it halfway up the transom, where it broke off and swam away. *Dang that Bobby Loomis!* I thought, before taking my angst out on Leroy.

"I felt bad about knocking your last salmon off," I said, "but your inability to get the net ready for my fish trumped that shortcoming."

Leroy counterpunched with the skill of a sparring partner who had seen it all. "I needed a knife to cut the weight, and mine was in another pair of pants. You should have given me yours."

By mid-morning, I was spent. Strikes had dropped off from regular to infrequent, and the constant dodging and weaving among boats was stressful. With eight fresh sockeye on ice, in addition to the four caught the afternoon before, we felt like we had given it our all. "Let's hang it up," Leroy said. "We've got one day's limit in total. That's more than I expected."

"I'm good with that," I replied. "We've had more than our share of action. Unfortunately, our skills were not always up to the challenge."

That's when Leroy looked at his watch and remarked, "It's been 24 hours since we left your house."

"Too much togetherness," I replied. "I might have to take your phone number off speed dial until after Christmas."

"I agree," Leroy replied. "Given the madness that we experienced today, I don't expect to think about you again until after I eat my last sockeye fillet."

That's the beauty of our relationship. Leroy and I know when it's time to take a break from the other, and neither of us minds saying so. If it wasn't for that darn shrimp salad, I would have been able to put him out of my mind for another month or so.

one more LAST CAST

GUINEA HEN STEELHEAD

THE WAY GRANDPA HARRY told it was Grandma Laura requested he "rustle up some fresh meat for chicken potpie."

"I only had two roosters in the flock at the time," he said. "You need at least two roosters in case a skunk gets into the coop and picks one off, so I wasn't going to wring either of their necks. And the hens were broody. I couldn't see messing with that. My idea was to poach one of the neighbor's guinea hens instead."

My interest was piqued. I knew Grandpa Harry was a rascal, but I didn't think he would cross the line. He continued, "The neighbor had a dozen or so birds. Figuring he wouldn't miss one, I grabbed my .22, shoved a handful of shells in my pocket, and headed down to the south pasture. I peeked through the fence and there, on the other side of the pond, was a nice, plump guinea hen. I snuck up within about 10 yards or so before the dang bird spotted me and hid behind a big log covered with blackberry vines. I crouched down, waited a spell, and sure enough, it stuck its fool head up to take a peek. That's when I took careful aim and fired.

Bang! A clean kill on a head shot, as near as I could tell.

But before I could get up, that dang bird raised its head again, so I shot once more. Surely this time I hit it, I thought, but no, its goofy head bobbed up again like an apple in a pail of water. About that time I was getting aggravated. I shot four more times. Each time, except the last, the bird's head went down behind the log and bobbed back up as if to look where the shot came from. Fool bird! Well, I waited for a minute or so after that last shot, just to make sure, before concluding I had finally bagged a guinea hen for your grandma's pot pie. But what happened next was the strangest thing. When I walked over to retrieve my bird, there were six guinea hens lying there on the ground behind the log. All shot clean through the head."

Grandpa's story flashed in my mind when a six-pack of fat-bodied guinea hens ran out from behind a small tool shed and frantically circled my truck like I was their long-lost relative. I had just turned into the graveled driveway of a small, two-story farmhouse set back from Highway 24. It was the first property upstream of the massive grain elevator that towered over the Touchet River at the intersection of Lyons Ferry Road. The Touchet is the largest tributary of the Walla Walla River, a little sister in terms of size, which originates from the north flanks of the Blue Mountains. My plan was to sneak in a few casts for steelhead before settling down in front of a home television to watch Super Bowl XLIV.

The farmhouse was old and dilapidated. Broken side windows were boarded up with faded plywood, the clapboard siding was in need of a fresh coat of paint, and the front porch leaned badly. It appeared abandoned except for a recent-model Buick sedan nosed up to the trunk of a gnarled black locust that had been planted several decades past to provide shade.

Getting out of my truck, I felt the usual trepidation that welled up in my gut when I approached an unknown outcome. Lolling on a torn piece of shag carpet was a large, gray tomcat. A tail-wagging Labrador retriever peered through a part-open screen door as if to back it up. I knocked on the weathered doorframe and wondered what to do if no one answered. There were faint footsteps, but it was several minutes before a shapely, bathrobe-clad woman came to the door. Her dishwater-blonde hair was neatly brushed but her eyes were puffy and half-shut. Although there was an air of attractiveness about her, on that winter day she exuded a look of, "Why bother, since life has dealt all the cards?"

"Good morning," I said. "I was wondering if I could fish on your property?"

"I'm only a renter," she replied. "You'll have to speak to the land owner if you want to fish here."

"Do you have his name?" I asked. "I'd like to contact him."

She paused as if to evaluate whether I was worth the trouble before disappearing into the house. When she returned, she handed me a scrap of paper with two phone numbers scribbled in #2 pencil. "The first one is for Bert, the son, and the other is for old Bert, the owner," she said. After I thanked her, she added, "I don't have a problem myself," and closed the door before I got ideas about her granting access to something other than a place to fish.

I returned to my truck and pretended to use a cell phone I didn't have before driving downstream of the property and parking next to two official-looking signs. One read "No Authorized Vehicles Behind This Sign" and the other, "Hunting By Written Permission Only." While neither sign invited, they implied a polite angler was not likely to be arrested for trespassing. I also figured that neither Bert would be checking the status of their winter wheat on Super Bowl Sunday.

My route to a stand of cottonwood that demarked the river led through a tangled jungle of reed canary grass and willow. On the way, I flushed three hen pheasants, spooked a white-tailed doe, and fell in a muskrat hole. Falling down is something I've gotten used to when trampling river bottomland. It comes with the territory. So far, the only thing I've injured is my pride.

The lower Touchet River consists of a series of slow-moving oxbows with deep-cut banks of dark topsoil. In most places, farmland is tilled up to stream bank, often leaving only a narrow band of willow and reed canary grass to contain the flow. Wading can be treacherous where silt has built up to create quicksand-like conditions. Avoiding such areas, I found an open section of rocky shoreline and cast to where cobble had built up on the inside of a bend to create a deep run.

Five casts later, I found myself hung up on a tree root. I broke off, tied on a new rig, and elected to map the bottom more intelligently. Warming to the task at hand, I worked the edge of a drop-off, a tailout, and a deep hole under a log. Unfortunately, imagination often exceeds reality. Regrouping, I threaded a fresh night crawler onto my hook and hiked upstream to a bend in the river. A shallow riffle butted into a steep mud bank to create a honey hole with sufficient depth and complexity to attract a steelhead.

I approached the situation like a shortstop honing in on a pop fly. The tailout did not reward, nor did the inside pocket where current slowed. *Time to test the sweet spot,* I thought. Pinching on extra split shot, I cast into the deepest part. My rig slid across the bottom, caught in current and ticked against a submerged boulder. That's when a fish grabbed it. Three headshakes later, my dormant reflexes were called into action. I set the hook on a fish that ran upstream before turning back to the security of deeper water. One short run later, I eased a small 1-salt hen to shore and removed the hook while she lay gasping in the shallows.

Her gleaming silver side contrasted with a gunmetal-gray back. Freckled spotting covered a broad, square tail. Her dorsal fin was wrinkled, and a smooth scar was visible where the flag of an adipose fin once protruded. A hatchery steelie. Contemplating the volume of fish already stored in the home freezer, I turned her around to compete with the genes of unclipped steelhead.

I fished several more holes without success until I reached a long, straight stretch of river that lacked character. Wisps of ground fog drifted eerily around an orange celestial ball that was sinking fast above sculpted hills of ancient flood-deposit loess. I rested on a senescent mound of reed canary grass and watched a red-tailed hawk coast down the river plain.

The air had turned damp and musty. I broke down my rod and headed for the truck.

With no fish to mess with, I had time to lay a fire in the living room fireplace before Super Bowl kickoff. The thought of whether to bag a plump guinea hen for a potpie also entered my mind.

one more LAST CAST

ON BEING SECOND-RATE

LIKE MOST LITTLE LEAGUE baseball players, I aspired to a professional career. I fueled my passion watching Willie Mays make basket catches on Saturday afternoon television. Using a high leg kick like Juan Marichal, I mixed up a 50-mph fastball with a sweeping nickel curve when I was ahead on the count. I led the league in hitting and was fearless on the base path. Few opponents had skin thick enough to ignore my incessant yammer in the field. Being chosen for the regional All-Star team merely affirmed what I had known all along. I was good!

What followed was a rude awakening. When I was grouped with select players from larger towns, I was no longer special. My skill on the base path was only adequate when compared to others graced with more speed. My bold play in the field was merely within range. Plus, many peers hit for power, while I hit for average. In the blink of an eye, I went from being the best baseball player in my hometown to a second-stringer competing for position. This reality came to pass despite the fact that

I had tossed baseballs through a tire hung from the backyard crabapple tree since I was five years old. My adolescent world would have been shattered except for a judicious upbringing.

This brief introduction serves as prelude to my life as an angler. All appearances suggest I am consumed by fishing. A "Gone Fishing" doormat greets you at the front door stoop. Pictures of salmon, steelhead, trout, bass, sturgeon, and walleye grace my office wall. The bathroom calendar is by Trout Unlimited. Historical fish art adorns the hallway, and my personal library showcases a collection of great fishing novels. There is more fish paraphernalia scattered about the house than you can fit on the back of a flatbed truck.

It's not all illusion. I was hooked on fishing from the moment I caught my first trout. I have fished for any species that can be eaten—and others that are better served up as crab bait. I have caught fish in places where others have tried and failed. I have caught fish on the first cast of the day and by the light of the moon. There is a fishing hole on the Hanford Reach of the Columbia River named after me. At this same location, I had someone declare (after watching me catch a steelhead and a Chinook salmon on successive casts) they would happily put a pair of underpants over their head if I suggested that doing so would help them catch a fish.

In my mind, I was an ace angler. That is, until I experienced the second great revelation in my sporting life. As I recall, the insight took hold on a steelhead fishing trip with GM. Until then, I had been stuck on the concept that, whether due to luck, skill, or a blessed combination of both, I was the best steelhead fisherman around.

Our route to the Tucannon River traced from Highway 124 on Lyons Ferry Road, a 45-mph county byway that leads to the lower Snake River near Little Goose Dam. There is no riding the shoulder because the edge of the road is either open range or a wheat field where asphalt merges with broken ground, so I straddled the centerline at 60 mph and split the difference on curves, like an Olympic skier going for gold. Silhouetted against a low ridge to the west of the road, a rough-legged hawk soared above bunch grass the color of wheat straw. When the big raptor hovered to eyeball a patch of scrub brush, I remarked to GM, "That's a lazy boy."

"Not necessarily," GM replied, following up with a story about a trip on the Madison River. "There was this guide who worked his drift boat oars slowly and surely whenever he approached a slot that provided opportunity. The approach related more to economy of motion as opposed to laziness."

Touché. Apparently, less effort is required when you know what you're doing. Another way of looking at it is that biding your time can improve your success rate. Meanwhile, I have spent much of my life looking for reason to float with my eyes closed when I should swim with purpose. Upon further reflection, the brief exchange served as a painful reminder of how hard I have to work to get exceptional results.

We motored north until the road dropped to view the lower Snake River Canyon. I turned right on Highway 261 at Lyons Ferry and proceeded upstream along the Tucannon River past the town of Starbuck, where I parked at the edge of a public access area. After grabbing our gear, we walked single file on a well-trodden path through cattail and reed canary grass. By the time we reached the alder over-story, GM was in a zone, his intensity fueled from the ever-present wad of tobacco tucked in his lower lip.

I've only chewed tobacco once. It was after a high school baseball game in nearby Dayton. More than 40 years ago. As I recall, we lost 6 to 3 to a superior team, and I rode in the back of a yellow school bus on the hour-long drive back to Weston. Second baseman Rodney passed around a can of Copenhagen and we all took a pinch. "Hold it between your cheek and gums with your tongue," he said. "You get a good buzz."

Why not? I thought. *You'll never make it to the majors if you don't know how to chew tobacco.* I held the pinch tight to my molars while nicotine did its thing on my dilettante nervous system. Unfortunately, there was no chance to spit before the coach sensed something was going on. "I hope you guys know that any kind of tobacco use is breaking training," he said, pacing up and down the aisle to look each of us in the eye.

Nobody said a word. We did our best to look as innocent as white sugar on milk toast. Coach eventually returned to his seat, but eyed us for the next 40 miles of slow bus driving. Meanwhile, my stomach churned and my head spun from tobacco juice I couldn't help but swallow. A 20-minute hot shower at the gym helped ease my light head, but it took a bowl of chicken noodle soup and a good night's sleep to feel normal. As a consequence of that unsavory experience, I vowed never to chew tobacco again.

Back on the Tucannon River, I watched GM approach a slow, deep run, sizing it up through polarized lenses before he took a cast. It wasn't five minutes before he'd hooked and landed a small, bright hen. Unfortunately, the fish came in snagged on its left pectoral fin. "A lazy hookset," he said, knowing that foul-hooked fish don't count when it comes to bragging rights.

I switched bait after GM landed a second fish, this one a small, dark hatchery buck with pearly white gums. Meanwhile, I lost a steelhead that came to the surface at the sting of my hook, shook its head and was off. An even lazier hookset, I figured.

When GM moved alongside, I pointed out where I'd hooked my fish, elaborated on other potential holding areas and shared my thoughts on fish behavior. He did not respond, but I didn't take it personally. GM rarely conversed when there were fish to be caught. It's almost like he figures he'll miss an opportunity if he isn't giving it his all. *Then again, he was high on nicotine, so what do I know?* In contrast, I allow my mind to drift off track, like a cluster of roe cast to the wrong part of a drift.

Inspired by possibility, I added an inch of pencil lead to my drift rig and cast to the deepest part of the pool, where strong current swirled against exposed alder roots. *Perhaps our activity had pushed fish to cover?* As if on cue, a steelhead hammered my Corky and plowed back and forth in a series of short runs. When it tired, I steered it like a water-soaked log towards the bank. It was a deep-body, two-salt hatchery buck with flanks splashed crimson red. *Good for me,* I thought. *It's now one to one, but who's counting?*

Our next stop was near Starbuck, where GM had knowledge of private property deemed okay to fish. We ignored a "No Tres-passing" sign strung from a three-strand barbed-wire fence and headed upstream. I stopped on a high, clay bank to study a deep drift while GM crossed to the other side. Looking my way, he motioned if I wanted to share the hole, but overhanging brush put me on the wrong side of the river. "Have at it!" I yelled, and headed upstream.

Giving the hole away was a bad decision. No sooner had I settled into a casting rhythm than I heard a wolf whistle and glanced up to see a steelhead do a double flip in midstream. GM chased downstream and disappeared. With him out of sight, my attention returned to a series of pools created by basalt boulders placed along the opposite bank. I remember feeling second-rate, down two fish to one.

Another whistle soon followed. Distracted by the notion of a steelhead on the end of a line that wasn't mine, I ripped a hole in my waders climbing over a barbed-wire fence. GM soon appeared from the brush, showing off a small hatchery buck. "I released the other one," he said. "It was a wild hen."

By now, rain was coming down in sheets. We bailed for the refuge of my truck, where GM shared that he'd had enough action. "I can take the boys to soccer practice if we head back now," he explained.

The announcement created an uncomfortable situation. I had planned to fish until time for supper. More importantly, I needed to catch another steelhead to round things out. After some negotiation, we compromised to fish the first highway bridge, then head home. My ace in the hole was, "He who drives decides when to quit fishing."

This time we split up. *Just one more steelhead and I will be happy*, I thought, as I approached a deep run shaded by overhanging alder. Casting to where the current swelled dangerously close against exposed tree roots, I let my Corky swing into a slow pocket. It settled to the bottom, stopped, and I felt tension. That was it. No grab, no pull, no subtle "tick, tick," no "chunka, chunka, chunka." The steelhead was just on. After a short battle I slid a 4-pound hatchery buck to shore. *Good. Two keepers. That puts me back in the game.* I headed back to my truck.

GM was not in sight, so I sat on the tailgate, polished off a warm PBR, and reflected on the surroundings. Passing semitrucks splashed rain off asphalt. The pungent odor of decaying vegetation filled the air. Clouds raced up the river valley. Quail twittered anxiously from the brush.

Tired of waiting, I drove up and down the road, honking my horn. It was two passes before GM scrambled up the bank with a steelhead hanging from a short piece of rope. "I had one hit right at my feet and missed it, but threw it back in and hooked this one on the next cast," he said.

Some things only make sense after a series of hard knocks are applied to the top of your head. Others come to you quick and easy. That day on the Tucannon River included insight of both types. As it turned out, GM was the All-Star angler and I was merely competing for a position. It was the kind of experience you don't forget. Like chewing tobacco and having no place to spit.

one more LAST CAST

CRANKY MOTORS

THE FIRST TIME A CRANKY boat motor compromised a fishing trip with Leroy was on the lower Snake River. As I recall, he promised to show me a secret trolling location for steelhead near Ice Harbor Dam. "Released one wild and caught two keepers in less than two hours," he bragged.

No sooner had we put in at Charbonneau Park than the day unraveled. Leroy's 90-horsepower Mercury outboard wouldn't turn over and we couldn't figure out why. "I don't understand it," he said. "I charged the battery last night."

"Regardless," I replied, after jiggling color-coded wires for 20 minutes, "things appear deader than a doornail."

Two-foot-high whitecaps rolled upstream with a prevailing southwest breeze but we both wanted to fish really bad, so we fired up his ancient kicker in hopes it would power us across the river. The kicker died before we'd navigated 100 yards, but we managed to creep back to the launch with the aid of a spare oar.

I forgave Leroy for the debacle after I landed a bright,

10-pound hatchery hen next to the launch using his spare shrimp-and-bobber rig. In contrast, he didn't find forgiveness in his heart for what happened a few years later during a spring walleye trip to Lake Rufus Woods.

Knowing Leroy's penchant to criticize, I readied my Smoker Craft like a quality assurance manager prepares for a government audit. I charged the main battery and a spare. I filled the gas tank, checked function of all instrument gages and tested the kicker motor to make sure it ran smoothly. Life jackets were stowed. Insurance and registration papers were accounted for. In a rare demonstration of due diligence, I cleaned old fish blood and slime off the gunwales.

Unfortunately, my efforts were wasted at the Seaton's Grove launch. The starter motor stuck when I backed the boat off the trailer and flames erupted from the instrument panel. I frantically tried to disconnect the battery cable, but by the time I shut the motor off, the wiring harness was a molten mass of copper and multi-colored plastic.

So there we were, 160 miles from home, saddled with a broken-down boat and with three days of planned fishing in front of us. Luckily, the rest of our fishing party soon arrived. With some negotiation, Leroy and I managed to hitch a ride on separate boats.

The afternoon finished on a high note when I caught three eater-sized "eyes" as darkness fell on Buckley Bar. Unfortunately, when my crew met up with others at the launch, Leroy was nowhere to be found. "What happened to Leroy?" I asked Corey.

"He wasn't catching anything and wanted to troll," Corey said. "But I told him to quit whining. It was jigging or nothing.'"

I looked up the road to where my broken-down boat was parked. Standing in the shadows was a solitary figure with his head down. As I approached, a morose Leroy said, "I want to go home. It's not working for me."

"Go home?" I replied. "But I've already paid for the motel! Not to mention we have two more days of walleye fishing in front of us. Hey, don't fret. Tomorrow will be better."

"Sorry, but I don't want to fish with those guys again. Bob's okay, I guess, but I don't have anything good to say about Corey. Besides, I've already figured out I can drive your boat and trailer home if you hitch a ride back. That way, you can stay and fish with your buddies."

Although Leroy's solution to his plight was sound, it posed a dilemma. Nobody wants their fishing buddy to go home early. However, I figured the odds were good he would change his mind after a few beers, so I replied, "Let's sleep on it and see how you feel in the morning."

As things turned out, we woke up to 50-mph winds and had to cancel the rest of the trip. Walleye fishing is all about boat control, and boat control is difficult when waves crest over your bow. Leroy and I drove back together as originally planned and all was forgotten—until two years later, when the seal on my boat trailer wheel blew on the 3-hour drive to Lake Pateros for summer Chinook salmon. The end result was waiting for a tow truck by the side of the road on a triple-digit August afternoon. Although my boat trailer was fixed the next day, Leroy remained too nonplussed to rearrange his schedule for another try. "I need a break," he said.

Needless to say, the experience made his "Bottom 10" list of fishing trips for the year. In contrast, a more recent trip to Brewster (in Leroy's boat this time) started off great when I hooked and landed a sockeye immediately after I dropped my Smile Blade rig down to the chosen depth. Unfortunately, his ancient kicker motor coughed and died on the second pass through the same 50-foot-deep hole that appeared loaded with sockeye targets. "I think it's overheated," Leroy said.

"After 10 minutes on the water?" I replied. "How old is that motor, anyway? You make too much money to own a kicker you can't depend on."

Following a series of futile attempts to revive his ancient kicker, Leroy hooked up his bow-mount. "I've got two good batteries," he said. "There should be enough juice to last us until noon tomorrow."

"As long as the wind doesn't blow," I said under my breath.

Unfortunately, his trusty bow-mount would only turn to the left. Inability to steer is a problem when you are surrounded by a hundred other boats. Getting T-boned while you drive in circles comes to mind.

The end result was that Leroy moved to the bow and perched on a 20-quart Coleman cooler to manually control boat speed and direction while I managed our rods and shouted depth and fish target information. On regular occasion, I reminded Leroy of the importance of having a functional motor when you troll for salmon. He rebutted that I had no complaint, since we were catching fish. "The point is not experiencing adversity, it's rather how you deal with it," he said.

Leroy had a valid point. Going home with a cooler full of salmon added up to an excellent trip, especially when your ability to perform is handicapped by a pair of cranky motors. Further criticism was kept close to the vest, however. As my mother so often reminded, "If you can't say anything nice, then don't say anything at all."

DARAN'S ROD

IT'S FUNNY HOW siblings, not so far apart in years, pursue different sports. My big brother Daran set other interests aside in his early 20s to pursue a career in golf. Although he never played on the PGA tour, he received numerous plaudits as a teacher. I remained the crazy fisherman in the family. Not until late in life did we fish together, as practiced in our youth. Because Daran's bad hip precluded him from hiking with fly rod in hand, we opted to fish out of my boat.

Daran had the patience of a saint when it came to waiting for a strike from lock-jawed salmon. I couldn't help but think he'd developed his remarkable staying power overseeing the inept swing of beginning golfers on the practice range. For example, when I would inquire, "Want to change your lure?"

He would almost always reply, "I like this one."

Meanwhile, I swapped out my gear every hour or so, hoping to find that lucky combination.

Our benchmark fishing trip occurred the year before he was

diagnosed with an aggressive form of adenoid cancer. The morning began with a snot-clearing, kidney-jarring ride into the heart of the Hanford Reach of the Columbia River. With wind blowing hard from the southwest, the ride back to the launch was slated to be worse.

Our first stop was near Selph Landing, where we back-trolled sardine-wrapped Kwikfish behind a lead ball dropper. It was inside of an hour when Daran's patience was finally rewarded. "There's a solid strike," I said when his rod tip jerked violently. Daran struggled to his feet and wrestled the rod from the holder as line peeled from his level-wind. "Looks like a derby winner!" I yelled.

Unfortunately, our excitement was short-lived. Daran thumbed down on the fast-moving spool and snapped his 25-pound test leader at the swivel. "What did you do?" I asked, in a tone that admonished more than supported.

"It was taking all my line," he replied with chagrin.

All I could think of was, *the big one got away.* "That's what salmon do," I said. "They take off at the sting of the hook. Assuming it was well-hooked and the drag was set correctly, all you had to do was keep steady pressure until it tired. But don't worry, the odds are good we'll get another fish."

We moved upriver to Taylor Flats, where I hooked a salmon of my own. Not until I led the fish close did I sense that Daran had not been educated in the fine art of netting. The fish was large, maybe 20 pounds, and still green. Adding to the challenge was a blinding glare on the water and a stiff breeze that blew the boat sideways. Rather than scoop the salmon up when I brought it to the boat, Daran dropped the net frame on the salmon's head, effectively "trapping" it. His attempt would have been forgivable except that my Kwikfish got tangled in the net mesh.

After observing the back hook firmly embedded in the salmon's jaw, I stretched over the gunwale to work the net frame under the moribund fish. Unfortunately, my frantic effort dislodged the jaw hook and our second derby winner of the day slipped down into the emerald-green depths of the Columbia River.

It wasn't until respite was gained from the wind that Daran redeemed himself following yet another takedown. This salmon he fought with resolve before matter-of-factly remarking, "It's off."

"Keep reeling." I said. "Sometimes they swim toward the boat when they first get hooked."

Daran took direction to find the salmon still on. "It's pulling pretty good, but I don't think it's as big as the last one," he said.

He was correct. The salmon wasn't very big. However, putting a salmon in the box is never a bad thing, even if it's small and not so bright. "Looks like a buck," I said when I netted it. "It should cut good."

I gave Daran a new casting rod and reel of his own that Christmas and planned to train him on proper netting technique. "We'll get you a fish next year," I promised after our annual trip for Chinook salmon came up dry. "Maybe you can come up later in the season when fishing gets better."

But the next season never happened. Daran was too weak following a second round of chemo to make the 200-mile drive from his home in Portland. "Maybe Dusty can bring you up," I said. "Between the two of us, we can load you in the boat and prop you up for a few hours of trolling."

But Daran argued against the wisdom of it, being the most conservative (and practical) member of the family.

That winter was one of the most difficult periods in my life. My siblings and I traded off visits to allow Daran to remain home rather than get "farmed out"—as he put it—to a terminal care facility. While my sisters concentrated on proper nutrition, I focused on providing a good time. If he woke up feeling like buttermilk pancakes soaked in maple syrup, I served up a short stack made from scratch. If he was interested in action-adventure cleavage, we watched cable TV until he nodded off in his faithful La-Z-Boy recliner. Playing golf and fishing were off the list, but watching the latest PGA tournament or the boys on *Hawg Quest* whoop it up allowed us to pretend.

Daran slipped away in the spring of 2012. I felt his last pulse, remaining at his side until he was taken away, and spent a lonely night next to his empty bed. Only when we sorted through his possessions was my consolation prize revealed: a nearly new salmon rod and reel tucked away in the corner of his garage. The unfair part was that Daran took a boat ride to heaven before he caught a salmon on it.

I fished by myself the first time Daran's casting rod found action. Taking advantage of a two-pole endorsement, I flat-lined a bright-orange Magnum Wiggle Wart off his spinning rod and back-trolled a chartreuse Spin-n-Glo sweetened with roe off my favorite Ugly Stick. Each cast of the Wart began with, "Let's catch a fish, bro."

Later that season, while fishing for fall Chinook salmon with my other brother, Dusty, I repeated the same tactic. Wouldn't you know it; Daran's rod soon jackhammered to the tune of a big salmon. Only when the salmon got close did I notice that the trailing hook of the Wart was embedded in its dorsal fin. "Dang it, bro," I said. "Looks like a salmon whacked your Wart and missed. Sorry, but this one doesn't count."

About this time, I sensed Dusty's discomfort with the conversation I was carrying on with our dearly departed brother, but I persevered. "That's the first salmon landed on Daran's rod," I explained. "He doesn't care if it was foul-hooked. Actually, he would have, but I don't. It's better than nothing."

Nonetheless, we released the large Chinook with mixed feelings. However, rules are rules, and you must abide by them or the world will collapse into anarchy.

Two days later, I returned to the same section of river with my neighbor, Dick. Once again, I strung up Daran's rod and tossed the lucky orange Wart out the back of the boat. "Come on, bro. Let's catch a fish!" I yelled.

It was an hour before Daran's rod went down in response to the strike of an aggressive salmon. After a short but spirited fight, we netted a toothy, 10-pound buck. "It's a keeper," I said, beaming with pride. "It's Daran's first legitimate salmon on his casting rod!"

Unlike Dusty, Dick was unfazed by my come-back-from-the-dead talk. "I can only guess that your big brother is smiling down on us," he replied.

one more LAST CAST

SIX COLORS

"THE MOST RECENT postings for Area 19 said they let six colors out," Tim said.

"What's a color?" I replied, knowing it's often better to admit you don't know what the other person is talking about before they get too deep into the topic.

"Lead core line comes in different colors," he explained. "Each color is for 10 yards of line."

"I've never used leaded line," I said, "but I get it. That's a lot of line, though. Why don't you fish off a downrigger or add weight instead?"

"Everyone says you need to troll 150 to 200 feet behind your boat. That's why."

Tim and I were planning a day trip to Lake Roosevelt. After being thwarted by road ice and high winds the year before, I looked forward to experiencing the famous winter fishery for rainbow trout. I'd been looking at pictures of anglers on the Internet holding up large, silver-bright fish for over a month. Tim, a veteran of over a dozen trips to the Fort Spokane area, explained that we would troll an oversized Keda fly behind either a dodger or wedding ring spinner. "Some anglers tip the fly with a worm," he said. "Others add one or two kernels of canned corn soaked in garlic scent."

It was a Saturday morning in mid-January when we arrived at the launch following a three-hour, white-knuckle drive over black ice and snow. A dense layer of fog lifted around noon to reveal the first blue sky in a month. I carefully spooled line from my Penn level-wind: black, gray, red, brown, purple, green. I may be partially red-green colorblind, but I can count to six in three different languages. It seemed so simple, yet fishing three rods out the back of Tim's Hewescraft did not produce a single takedown in the same area that had yielded boat limits for him before.

Were fish driven deep, spooked by the dazzling sunlight in crystal clear water? Or did recent lowering of the reservoir cause fish to move towards the dam, as one angler alluded to when we inquired about his luck at the dock? Regardless, our day yielded but one strike in four hours of trolling. With no fish to brag about on the long drive home, Tim and I speculated on technique, reservoir elevation, and the possible effects of sunlight on trout behavior. That we might have been inept never came up.

Undaunted by the humbling experience, I returned to Lake Roosevelt a week later with two friends. Like my Uncle Chuck used to say, "You've got to pick yourself up off the ground, get back on that pony and ride."

Ken and Ted, both avid fly fishers, had tied up a dozen marabou flies based on Tim's store-bought versions. All colors of the rainbow were represented. Some patterns were enhanced with beads and tinsel. Some had trailing stinger hooks. To supplement their fly collection, I brought a tackle box full of gear similar to what anglers had posted on the Internet. We had two bait casting outfits along with two leaded line outfits that Tim loaned us. I was excited and confident about the possibilities.

Since reports said trout moved lower in the reservoir during the winter drawdown period, our plan was to fish close to Grand Coulee Dam from the Spring Canyon launch. I reserved a lakeside kitchenette unit at the Sky Deck Motel in Electric City, where we were one of only two parties at the motel. "It's too early for walleye fishing," the desk clerk said when we checked in, "but we've got 12 groups coming this weekend.

Thursday afternoon started off with two solid strikes in the first hour, both on a red Wiggle Wart flat-lined off the middle rod. The second strike resulted in a fat, 17-inch rainbow that Ted led to the net. "The skunk is off," I said when we gave each other a high five, thinking the best was to come. However, it wasn't to be. The rest of the day did not produce so much as a bump.

"Electric City can reward in ways other than catching fish," I reassured my two bunkmates back at the Sky Deck. "Last time here, Ken and I rubbed shoulders with locals around a fire pit until midnight. Let's hike up the hill to the E-City Bar and Grill and check out the action."

Unfortunately, tavern patrons were subdued, and the outside fire pit was not in operation, so evening entertainment consisted of us shoving dollar bills into a jukebox that demanded extra credits from our '70s and '80s playlist. "Evidently you pay extra for guitar solos," I said after Ted had emptied his wallet of greenbacks. The only other matter of mention was stellar service by an ancient barmaid who responded to our jokes with a pirate-like, "Har, har, har, har."

We slept soundly in our two-queen-plus Murphy bed suite, the stillness of night punctuated by the occasional flatulence ascribed to old men who drink microbrews and eat greasy food. "So much for a view," I said when I pulled back the window shades at daybreak to reveal the Banks Lake shoreline blanketed by dense fog. That wasn't the worst of it. A cruel north breeze ruffled the Stars and Stripes, and the parking lot was a solid sheet of ice.

After a careful assessment of the situation, we opted to pull my boat 30 miles up-lake to Fort Spokane, where clear skies welcomed. Unfortunately, fishing there was more of the same. "I think people only post something when they catch fish," Ted said. "I bet nobody posts skunks."

"Either that or they make stuff up," I replied.

Absent a single takedown in over three hours, we stopped at the launch to take a restroom break. That's when I asked another angler, "What's the secret?"

"Some say fish have moved out because water levels have dropped," he replied, "but rainbows are lazy. They're still here, but closer to shore."

Taking a cue, we worked the shoreline. That's when Ken tied on a plastic side-planer advertised as being "the last one you'll ever use." *No wonder,* I thought, after observing the difficulty of rigging it up. Luckily, Ted interceded with written instructions and we were back in action with four rods fishing. Back in action, that is, until I made a figure-eight turn to vary lure action and Ken's lead line crossed Ted's. It took Ted half an hour to wrap the first 50 feet of snarled line around an empty beer can and consolidate the rest in a neat pile on the floor of the boat. Meanwhile, I lost two trout that struck two different Wiggle Warts fished at two different depths. Our lead-line rigs were still without a bump.

"You wasted valuable fishing time dealing with the mess," I said to Ted. "But to your credit, you hung in there. Don't worry. We can do without a fourth rod. Lead line wasn't working anyway."

"I didn't mind it so much," he replied. "The truth is, I feel pretty good right now. Somewhere between having sex and catching a fish."

In one final attempt to salvage the day, we jigged for walleye where the Spokane River arm emptied into the Columbia. I hooked a 12-incher, but neither fishing buddy was impressed. Despite best attempts to rationalize the fishing trip as an "adventure," it was difficult to categorize catching one trout and one shaker walleye as successful. Cranking up the volume on the CD player during the long drive home provided some consolation. As I recall, blues were the genre of choice. Like the DJ said, "Music about feeling real bad can make you feel good."

The next morning found me uncoupling the ankle-high mess of lead line left in the bottom of my boat. If it had been my outfit, I would have cut the line rather than deal with the mess. But it wasn't, and Tim wanted his outfit back. Meanwhile, I couldn't help but reflect on how frustrating it can be for a neophyte to fish a new location. You'd like to think you could gain insight into where and why trout reside—and maybe even catch a few fish, based on your past experience. That I spent the morning untangling line on the front lawn instead of packaging up red-meat fillets for the freezer said something about where I was on the learning curve for the Lake Roosevelt trout fishery.

The first step in outsmarting the loose stack of line required that I walk slowly backwards and check progress at regular intervals. *Where did this magnetic attraction come from?* The tedious process was a test of patience. A special challenge was presented each time the prior-mentioned beer can rolled loose to join the party. I eventually outsmarted the demonic line, however, relying on a deliberate approach that defied a life-long tendency towards attention deficit disorder.

When I finished, lead line from Tim's Penn 209M stretched across the lawn from the front curb to the back porch. Reeling in slack, I couldn't help but count the colors: green, purple, brown, red, gray, black. *Wouldn't you know? Six colors were out. At least we got something right.* And, it turned out that Ted was correct. There was a certain afterglow associated with the act of untangling lead line.

SHUFFLEBOARD EXCURSION

EVEN THE BEST-PLANNED outings can turn out to be a fiasco. Case in point was a February excursion with Leroy for B-run steelhead on the Clearwater River. In hindsight, I did everything right. I blocked my calendar a month in advance and warned Nancy that I would be leaving her. I checked websites for information on steelhead run size, timing, and angler catch rates. I confirmed water conditions with a friend who worked at the Clearwater National Fish Hatchery. I worked up a batch of fresh bait, and put together an assortment of tried and proven lures.

As the weekend approached, daytime temperatures were projected to climb into the low 40s, and creel census reports showed a steady increase in catch rates. By all appearances, the trip was slated to be successful.

Back then, Leroy and I had fished together often enough to know we shared a passion for catching fish. That much was evident. But we hadn't gone on an overnight trip. As it turned out, extra time together tested our relationship in ways that I had not predicted.

The first hiccup occurred when Leroy's ancient 15-horsepower Johnson struggled to make headway past a gauntlet of boulders between the Pink House launch and Black Rock Hole. Although I knew Leroy got upset when things didn't go his way, the severity of his cussing outburst was impressive. However, that event was mere warm-up to a tantrum that occurred when another angler crossed his line. In a crazy demonstration of how not to disengage braided line, Leroy grabbed at the snarl and stuck himself on a laser-sharpened hook. I was quick to cut both rigs loose, being less concerned with losing $3.50 worth of gear than the geyser of blood spurting from Leroy's right index finger.

Despite pounding the water for six hours at locations that had produced steelhead for me in the past, day one went into the book as a skunk. Depressed but not demoralized, we returned to impressive accommodations at the Helgeson Place Hotel. Our $79 suite included one queen- and one king-size bed, full bath and kitchenette. The deluxe room package, advertised as "only $4 more than the standard," came with a 4-ounce screw-top bottle of Cabernet Sauvignon and monogrammed white terrycloth robes. Leroy and I slept soundly after drowning our sorrow with two pitchers of Moose Drool stout.

The morning arrived clear and bright following a heavy frost. After a leisurely breakfast, we attacked the half-inch layer of ice that was plated to his boat and truck windows. I recall thinking that Leroy was not fully engaged. In hindsight, I should have sensed that a storm was brewing.

Driving up North Fork Road, we found a smattering of anglers tossing drift bobbers from a riprap bank. Another lineup had gathered downstream along a fast water chute opposite the hatchery outfall. I rolled down the window to chat with an angler fishing off the Orofino Bridge. "How do you plan to land it?" I asked as he fought a steelhead from his position 100 feet above the water. He pointed to a steep path leading down to where a buddy stood with a long-handled net.

We continued to the Pink House launch to find the parking lot overflowing with boat trailers. Eight boats held position in the main drift where three boats had fished the afternoon before. "Looks like the Saturday morning crowd has mobilized," I said.

This fact did not go unnoticed by Leroy. Consequently, he nixed my plan to motor downstream to McGill. "Too many boats."

Regardless, I didn't give up on the idea. "Why don't we take a drive along the highway that parallels the river?" I suggested. "That way we'll get a feel for boat traffic."

Unfortunately, the road tour reinforced Leroy's opinion that my plan was too much trouble. "I could never make it back up the rapids with my little motor," he said. "You need at least a 25-horsepower motor to fish this river."

That's when I realized my vote didn't count. Even though I had planned the trip, it was Leroy's truck and Leroy's boat. So guess what? Leroy was calling the shots. Reinforcing that notion, he made an executive decision to drive back to Orofino to fish the South Fork arm. When I told him what I thought of the idea, he said, "You picked the place and method yesterday and we got skunked bigger than daylight. I'm going to pick the place and the approach today. We could do no worse."

I rarely keep remarks to myself, but in this case I bit my tongue because the only thing that came to mind was, "Up yours!" My only recourse was to retreat to a minimalist mode, avoid eye contact, and not speak unless spoken to. The situation quickly degenerated to that of an old married couple having different points of view on how to spend their money, but with neither having the pocket change to go shopping. There was one sore winner and one pissed-off loser in the game. When Leroy played his trump card, I tossed in my hand and let the cards fly loose for good measure. The dark side of our personalities had been exposed, the limits of friendship framed by the disagreement.

With Leroy at the tiller, we trolled mindlessly up and down the South Fork, oblivious that operations at Dworshak Dam had created more attractive flows for steelhead in the North Fork arm. The sun came out and charged my mental battery, but conversation remained limited to the occasional yup, nope, and okay. Never once did I hold hope of catching a fish, and the results matched that expectation. A bleached-out pile of filleted steelhead carcasses at the launch only confirmed what we had been hearing, "You should have been here last week."

Relieved to close our tackle boxes and return home, we stopped at the first convenience store for a six-pack. Two hours later found us out of beer and at the Tuxedo Tavern in Prescott, where I offered to buy burgers to even out that Leroy bought sand shrimp. Meanwhile, conversation had evolved from polite to jovial with the aid of alcohol.

The Miller Lite sign behind the bar emitted a soft glow to the dark wood interior. Dishes clattered in the kitchen and the smell of greasy fries filled the air. A trio of regular stool-sitters in matching blue satin bowling jackets sipped glasses of tap beer at the counter. I stepped up to the cash register and ordered two Jason burgers (the house special) without looking at a menu. Shoved against the north wall was a vintage tournament-size shuffleboard table, National Shuffleboard Company c. 1949.

I had played shuffleboard at the Tuxedo Tavern several times in the past, but on that afternoon, it exuded different karma. The playing surface was scratched and badly worn. Its purple felt gutter lining was torn, and half the scoreboard lights were burned out. Three of six pucks lacked their colored plastic insert.

Leroy and I gathered up loose pucks, sprinkled Sun-Glo on the board surface to speed up action and made a few practice shoves. Halfway through the first game, the tavern owner appeared from the shadows. "Are you the guy that is going to buy the shuffleboard?" he asked, when I nodded his direction.

I was quick to respond. "No, but I was thinking about making an offer. It doesn't look loved anymore."

When he paused as if to analyze my remark, I made my first mistake. "How much were you asking?"

He deliberated for several seconds before replying, "I'd take $450."

I had no clue of the shuffleboard's value. Although more unique than a pool table, a shuffleboard requires more space to operate. Rewiring it would also be a challenge. Nonetheless, the price seemed reasonable for a vintage tavern game you don't see every day.

What happened next was as pure an experience as hooking and landing a 20-pound B-run steelhead from the Clearwater. Whether desperate for something good to happen or showing off, the situation posed a golden opportunity for something good on a day when nothing good had gone my way. I followed the owner back to the bar and asked, "Would you hold the shuffleboard until I figure out what to do with it?"

He wrinkled his thick black mustache, shuffled his feet and said, "Sure."

I put $50 down on my credit card to hold the board. The tavern owner wrote his contact information on the top portion of a food receipt and I wrote my mine on the bottom. He tore the receipt in half and in that manner, we completed the first step in the deal. Meanwhile, the oldest member of the bar stool trio eased off his seat to share what he knew about the board's history. "It was transported from a tavern in Walla Walla several years ago. The biggest problem getting it here was keeping it together when we drove over the railroad tracks."

I took a deep breath. What had I got myself into? One thing was for sure. I left the tavern with a fishing buddy more impressed than when the day started. Admittedly, several weeks passed before Leroy and I thought about fishing with each other. A four-beer buzz moves a relationship along only so far.

It was two weeks before the shuffleboard found a temporary home. Our 1,754-square-foot ranch-style house didn't have a game room or a basement, and the 22-foot-long shuffleboard would not fit in a two-car garage that held a vintage Austin Healey 3000 and Nancy's Acura. Luckily, GM stepped up with an offer to store it until I developed a long-term plan. "Using a garage for a car is a waste of good space," he said.

There are certain advantages to having an oversized garage that does not store cars. GM's pride and joy, a 19-foot Alumaweld, was parked in one garage bay. The other bay held a trio of upright freezers, mountain bikes, skis, recycling containers, and a table saw, among other practical and recreational equipment. The shuffleboard looked right at home when it was eased into the middle of it all.

A controversy was sparked, however, when GM's wife dictated, "Make the board playable or move it out." Several months later, with a foot of snow on the ground, I finished the first stage of restoration: a third coat of varnish applied inside a plastic tent whose interior temperature was elevated by a propane heater. After GM's father-in-law rewired the scoreboard lights, the shuffleboard was ready for prime time. Its presence provided a ready excuse to party, complementing GM's ready supply of home brew. It has been over seven years since that fateful weekend with Leroy, so I figure the shuffleboard will stay where it is. I'm also guessing GM figures it's his, and I tend to agree. Familiarity of use and common-law statutes transcend to certain rights of ownership after a period of time.

As for extended fishing trips with Leroy, the current arrangement is to trade off vehicles. That way nobody suffers from the other's despotic nature twice in a row. We've also learned the value of respecting the other's opinion. Unfortunately, some tipping points aren't revealed until after you pass the point of no return.

one more LAST CAST

GETTING YOUR DUE

CD AND I ARE NEARLY two decades apart in age, but we're bosom buddies when it comes to having fond memories of our alma mater. This collegial bond sets up an annual trip to fish for fall Chinook salmon in the Hanford Reach of the Columbia River. Despite the fact that we both have advanced degrees in fisheries science, we often struggle to put a salmon in the box. Until the Year of the Record Run, that is.

Prior to 2013, a year when over one million fall-run Chinook salmon entered the Columbia River, our most memorable trip involved a total of four salmon. As I recall, I landed the first fish, a bright, 20-pound hen, less than a half-hour after we started. After hooking a second fish, I passed the rod to CD so he could have fun with it. Unfortunately, CD failed to maintain a tight line when the salmon ran towards the boat and it got off. As I recall, his approach with the reel could be likened to someone afraid to hurt the fish's mouth.

Following the third take-down of the morning, I said, "I'm

going to fight this fish to the net, but you can have it."

CD's reply went something like, "Is it legal for you to do that?'

I said, "You bet it is. If it goes on my card, I'll be punched out and we'll have to head back to the launch."

As luck would have it, a fourth salmon succumbed to my lucky K-16 Double Trouble Kwikfish, and CD fought the salmon from beginning to end without mishap.

Faded memory of other trips includes catching few fish and feeling sorry for ourselves. But 2013 was different. To accommodate the huge surplus in salmon, fish managers had jacked up the daily limit. My confidence for an early October trip was high. Putting a dozen salmon on my punch card during the early part of the run helped in that regard.

After a brief exchange of e-mails, CD and I elected to meet at a start time designed to accommodate our morning constitution. Certain concessions must be made as you age. As one final check prior to departure, I tested the ignition key of my boat and found a dead battery. "I'm not sure what happened," I said. "Maybe I left the bow light on when I came down the river in the dark last week."

Although embarrassed, I did not panic. A spare battery was hooked up, the dead one put on charge, and a trolling motor battery grabbed as backup. "You sure are prepared," CD said, already forgetting my screw-up.

On the drive to the Snyder Street launch, CD shared that he planned to visit Susie Sockeye if we weren't successful. "Joanne wanted to be sure we had a salmon in the freezer this winter," he explained. "I'm not taking any chances after getting skunked last year."

I was reminded of his e-mail message the year before. "I weakened and bought a fish at Columbia Point Landing from a woman named Sockeye Susie who was selling Indian-netted Chinook from the back of a pickup truck. She was asking $4 per pound whole fish, $6 per pound gutted and headed, and $8 per pound filleted. I bought a 14.4-pound fish, whole, for $53."

I couldn't help but respond. "The math on your 14.4 pound fish does not work out. I think you bought the fish because you liked her name (and maybe more than that!)"

CD replied, "You were correct on the math. I got a bargain fish because Sockeye Susie was impressed with my good looks. She also gave me a small can of smoked salmon to seal the deal."

As things turned out, CD did not have to visit Sockeye Susie. Following a gut-wrenching, 20-minute boat ride over two-foot-high whitecaps, we back-trolled a shallow stretch of water near Ringold using Spin-n-Glos sweetened with golf ball-sized chunks of roe. My two-pole endorsement allowed me to flat-line a Magnum Wiggle Wart from a third rod out the back. A steady southwest breeze in combination with low flows challenged, despite having a relatively secluded stretch of river to ourselves. Consequently, I remained vigilant at the tiller, with the kicker motor throttled down to a whisper.

Less than five minutes passed before I hooked and landed a jack, causing CD to exclaim, "There you go. Catching all the fish again."

On the next drift, the Wart rod buckled and I brought a second salmon to the net. Perhaps recalling the earlier trip where: "How many fish can one person put on his punch card?" came into dispute, the brief flurry of action caused CD to inquire, "How many fish can we keep? Those darn regulations vary from area to area and change almost every week."

"According to the latest Emergency Rule notification, allowable sport harvest is three adults and three jacks apiece," I replied. "And we can keep fishing until the boat limit is reached. In other words, we can bonk a total of six adults and six jacks between us. But I wouldn't worry about us catching our limit with only two fish in the box."

Good fortune shifted to CD when he hooked and masterfully landed two nice salmon in successive drifts, a feat he ascribed to long-dormant skills surfacing. About then, I admit to wondering what he was doing that I wasn't. *Since when did all the salmon move to his side of the boat?* I put on my lucky roe-stained Oregon State University alumni sweatshirt and concentrated on my rod tip.

The next drift produced a hard strike when I reeled in the Wart to stow gear for another pass at the batch of biters. This hookset led to my second adult—a bright, 14-pound buck. Things heated up when both egg rods went down at once and our lines tangled. Only after my fish got off was I able to unravel the mess and coach CD with purpose.

"Keep your hand on the handle and don't stop reeling," I said. "You're milking it. If you don't keep a tight line, the fish will get off."

"I don't want to put too much pressure on it," CD replied. "It's bigger than the last one and I don't want to lose it."

As an aside, I must mention that CD can be stubborn when it comes to accepting advice from a former apprentice. For example, he once fished for American shad without success using a variety of lures of his own choosing before he tied on the "gold standard" Dick Nite Spoon I'd given him at the start of the day.

Back to the battle between CD and his salmon. Once encouraged, CD fought the big fish with resolve, although his ability to lead it to the net while I maneuvered the boat against a cruel crosswind was less than desirable. At least that's what I concluded after making a series of mad swipes at the backside of his fish.

As CD later explained, his style with the rod and reel had more to do with what he termed "fish-playing philosophy" than lack of skill. "I like to savor the moment, to let the fish play itself out before trying to land it," he said. "I learned that lesson the hard way when I fished for coho with Uncle Fred on Winchester Bay 70 years ago."

And he was on the right path. There's a lot that can go wrong if you try to horse a green fish to the net.

During one brief lull in the action, CD rested his backside on the cooler and remarked, "The trouble with catching all these fish is it's hard to remember much about their fight. It's all becoming a blur for me."

"A fish-catching orgy," I replied.

As things turned out, we ended the day with a double. Action commenced when CD barely raised his voice above a gentle whisper and announced, "Fish on." Apparently, strikes had become matter-of-fact.

I scrambled to reel in, but before I could get the middle rod out of the way, a salmon smacked the lucky orange Wart. Only after horsing a deep-bodied buck to the net and bonking it did I assist CD with his fish.

"That's it. We're done!" I exclaimed, after I netted his fourth salmon of the day—an all-time best. "We're tagged out!"

"I caught the biggest one," CD bragged after we laid all nine salmon on a sandy beach for a photo.

"Yes, you did," I replied.

"You caught more though," he said, with a twinkle in his eye. "No matter what, I figure this trip makes up for all the other times."

"I agree, but don't expect the same next year," I replied. "Us catching a limit of salmon is like our Beavers beating the Ducks in football. It's something that happens maybe once every five years. Regardless, I'm going to savor this day for a long time."

You could say we finally got our due.

ADDICTION

ONE HOT SUMMER night, my teenage son Matthew crawled out of his basement bedroom window after pretending to retire for the night. The source of his madness was a young temptress with waist-length black hair, a sweet smile and a body to match. "Matt will come through the front door sooner or later," I said to Nancy as I locked the latch to his window. She smoldered on the living room couch while I retired to sleep peacefully. What I didn't share was that I understood his situation because I had been there.

A similar lust overtakes me every year in late April. It's been that way ever since the spring run of Chinook salmon was restored to the Umatilla River. I grab my spinning rod, don my waders, and head for Chinaman's Hole. The thought of hooking a slab-sided, silver-bright salmon in small water makes my eyes glaze, my stomach churn, and my legs quiver. I admit it. I am an addict.

The first trip of the season begins with a burning sensation in the pit of my stomach and a mind that won't stop racing. Classical music tempers but does not relieve my angst. I can't help but worry how many anglers will be there, and if I can fish my favorite places. An addled brain once led to me making three false starts from my driveway. The first turn-around occurred when I forgot my Oregon fishing license. The second mishap involved a missing bag of ice and spare lead. I was 17 miles down the I-82 freeway the third time before I remembered leaving my waders hanging on a nail in the garage. Deep-breathing exercises were required to clear the head on that one.

The main source of my torment is a short stretch of water barely a stone's throw from the city of Umatilla. Along with being an angler's Mecca for world-class walleye, bass, sturgeon, salmon, and steelhead, the town is host to a grocery store with a 40-foot-tall parking lot cowboy, the now-closed More movie theater where the first eastern-Oregon showing of *Deep Throat* was presented in 1977, and the only strip joint within 200 miles. As far as Chinaman's Hole goes, the origin of the name is unclear. What is known is that placer mining and railroads brought over 3,000 Chinese to Oregon by 1880.

At the peak of salmon season, the shoreline of the river is littered with discarded bait containers, beer cans, plastic gloves, bottles, rotting fish entrails, and twisted bundles of monofilament. The nearby thicket of Russian olive harbors wood ticks and abandoned migrant worker camps. But aesthetics aren't everything. Like an old couch, Chinaman's Hole gets more comfortable with each visit.

Less than a mile up River Road is a graveled turnoff that holds a dozen vehicles. A narrow trail, overgrown with wild rose and reed canary grass, leads you down a steep bank to a pair of side channels that you must wade. Next to catch your eye is a dump-truck-sized pile of shot-rock rubble and castle-shaped basalt formations. You can't miss the centerpiece or the falls, where the river drops nearly six feet in elevation to eddy and surge like the ocean tide. The constant noise of falling water masks the sound of passing traffic and shouts of excited anglers. When spring Chinook salmon show on the lower Umatilla, I should be catching up on home-improvement projects. But I am either thinking about fishing or I am fishing. There's more. I tell lies to my wife and friends about where I am going and I cover up where I've been. My emotional state is as unstable as if I was involved in an illicit love affair.

Before I retired, I snuck off from work before the noon hour. By 1:00 p.m., coworkers thought I'd taken an early lunch. By 2:00 p.m., they figured I was in a meeting. As long as I returned to my desk before quitting time, nobody knew the difference. If I got skunked, I didn't say a word. If I was lucky enough to land a salmon, I waited a week before bragging. I didn't confide my exploits with even the closest of friends. There is a limit to how much you can trust others when it comes to having a good thing.

My addiction to springers can be traced back to the day GM handed me a map that showed where he caught two chrome-bright salmon. His Pictionary-like sketch included boulders, current lines, a partially submerged tree, and an "X" to show me where to cast. By the time I put the pieces of the puzzle together, I was almost out of bait. But luck was with me. My first cast towards the submerged tree put me fast into a salmon. The feeling was like holding a Brahma bull on a retractable leash. Unfortunately, my hook was dull from dragging on bedrock and the salmon swam free.

I have since learned that days at Chinaman's Hole play out like a chess match. Anglers shift position when a fish is hooked.

ɔomebody new arrives and wedges in. An opening is created when an angler leaves. Like urban neighbors, you are polite to those you share a property line with and you avoid eye contact with those who live across the street. In a male-dominated sport like bank fishing, casting for salmon is like peeing on a post. I've had egg clusters tossed close enough to shed water droplets on my baseball cap and bobbers land at my feet. Crossed lines are common, as is grousing about casting out of turn. Hold your ground or retreat. The choice is yours.

Challenges in casting etiquette aside, friendly banter helps fill the time. "I see you have custom waders," I said to a man who sported a pair of blue satin gym shorts over patched neoprene leggings. "Better than long johns, huh?"

Once you settle in, you find yourself giving spare tackle to unemployed mill workers, sharing heartfelt secrets with guys your spouse wouldn't allow past the front porch, encouraging anglers a neutered Labrador retriever would bite, and divulging secrets that took you years to acquire. Things nobody told you. Things you figured out after watching and waiting for hours.

An angler with a toothpaste smile spoke up after watching me land my second salmon of the morning. "I see where you were standing," he said.

"What's more important is where my bait ends up," I replied. "You can't get there from where you are casting."

Still, you don't wish for familiarity to cross the line to intimacy. As an example, I was once accosted as if I was an orange-vested attendant at Home Depot. "I bought this reel yesterday," the angler said as he sidled alongside. "They filled it with 20-pound monofilament line. I've spent more time fixing bird's nests than I have fishing."

His 3-ounce banana weight and 4/0 hook were more suited

for jigging rockfish than bouncing roe. I helped him adjust the drag and reminded him to slow the spool with his thumb before the lead weight hit the water. After wading off, I vowed to explain the merits of different gear if we met again. Meanwhile, I had a salmon to catch.

I am often reminded that fishing for springers is a lot like playing baseball. Not much happens between plays. You can chatter and you can daydream, but you had better be ready when play comes your way. It's one thing to hook a springer when you are alert and your senses are tuned. It's another when you have been lulled into complacency by hours of casting and the strike from a salmon ambushes like the sting of a maverick wasp. It helps me to imagine what a bite would feel like. Like when a ball of moss contacts your line and slides down like a fireman on a pole. Or when your slinky raps the top of a boulder during a fast water drift. Convincing others that a tug on your line is not due to moss, a rock outcrop or the nudge of a sucker is another worthwhile diversion.

"One was pecking on it."

"I just missed a solid gnash."

"That was for sure a pull-down."

Of course, your credibility is much higher when you have a salmon on the bank. It's like bluffing at poker. A big stack of chips proves you know what you are doing. Winners are far better at embellishing an experience than losers.

Hook a salmon only to lose it and you are nothing. Worse, you are lower than nothing because you blew it. Bad leader? Dull hook? Got tangled on a rock? Those excuses suck and so do you, if you elaborate to all within earshot. Lose two salmon in a row and you might as well change your name, wear a disguise, and don't come back. However, catch a springer and you are king for a minute, an hour, or maybe a day.

I waded onto a basalt shelf that diverted current one late April morning and cast a ball of roe into a deep plunge pool. *Wham!* My first springer of the season was on. The hank of orange yarn above my hook flashed in the current when the fish came top-water to hold position where divergent currents swelled. Adding drama were rock pinnacles capable of sawing off 20-pound test line, and uneven footing. I eventually backed up and worked the salmon to where an accommodating angler stood with a dip net. After netting my fish, he congratulated me with a thumbs-up handshake that I reciprocated due to having a former hippie peace-nik lifestyle. Unfortunately, he complicated the exchange with a pumped fist move that put me out of my element (although I managed to brush his knuckle). Some of us can't dance the Macarena with a DJ shouting instructions, let alone pull off a two-part handshake.

There was no compulsion to catch another salmon, but I wasn't going home while the sun shone brightly, redwing black-birds chortled, and cumulus clouds floated by. I was reminded of a recent dental appointment. A steady stream of nitrous oxide coursed through my veins while sharp instruments poked sensitive tissue. The feeling was euphoric, yet short-lived. When I described the experience to GM, he replied, "It's like riding the razor's edge."

A successful hookset with a springer creates a similar high. The only way to sustain the feeling is to hook another. As Leroy once said, "It's not about need, it's about greed."

So once the euphoria of that first fish wore off, I moved upstream to fish side by side with two anglers who proclaimed a missed strike on every fifth cast or so. Their boundless enthusiasm kept me entertained, optimistic, and alert. "I lost a

30-pounder in this hole yesterday," one said. "I used up all my eggs so I borrowed a shrimp. *Wham!* The salmon took it on the first cast. It looked like a tuna when it came out of the water."

Every year is different, though. On the last day of one unrewarding season, I rose in the low light of dawn after spending the night twisting and turning on a rumpled mattress. My catch card record did not include a single salmon, but I was determined to go down swinging. *It's not like I miss my face with a spoon when I eat cereal,* I thought as I waded into position and cast into the middle of Chinaman's Hole. The difference between that cast and a thousand others that year was a springer struck my baited hook with vengeance. It was a no-brainer bite that shook the cobwebs from my brain. The feeling was like cannonballing down a black diamond slope, riding the meanest bull in the rodeo (naked), grabbing onto the railing of a runaway train.

The battle immediately unleashed feelings of pent-up anxiety. *Do I have a good hookset? Is my drag set correctly? What about hidden snags?* Suppressing a dull ache in the pit of my stomach, I tried to quiet quivering legs and a racing mind. As if to emphasize the uncertainty, my spinning reel screamed each time the salmon made a powerful run. Only when its activity slowed and I considered where to land the fish did round two of hidden anxiety kick into full gear. *I hope it doesn't start rolling on me! Please, God, let my knots hold!*

I have always maintained that religion is there when you need it. Like the billboard by the side of the freeway reads, "Hell or Heaven. It's your choice." In this case, I chose heaven and steered the fish close, hoping to slide it onto the shore. But it took off like they do when the bottom closes in so I cranked down on the drag and led it back. As if by divine intervention, a watching angler arrived at my side with a net. My first and last springer of the year was soon secure.

So how do you overcome negative behavior that impacts your life and others? Compulsive behavior that includes preoccupation, impaired decision-making, and craving of the unattainable? You might dig deep within for a cure, but I am weak when it comes to quitting even the simplest of habits. One Schick Shadel advertisement reads, "Our aversion therapy causes the patient to reject the ever so powerful subconscious to overcome the thoughts of the conscious." Unfortunately, rehabilitation centers such as Schick Shadel treat alcohol, drugs, tobacco, and sex. Fishing is not on their list of cures. The closest thing to Springers Anonymous in my neck of the woods is the local fly casters club, and they don't relate to tossing bait.

According to clinical psychologists, the pull of addiction lessens when there is no longer a reward, when the cost of feeding the addiction exceeds the thrill. When it comes to springers, I quit fishing when I run out of bait or the season is closed. Like the actress Betty Davis said about her adulterous affair in the classic murder mystery *The Letter*, "It's like some loathsome disease, but I couldn't give it up."

I feel the same about springers, with the difference being I haven't killed anyone over it.

Why do I punish myself this way? Is it because spring mornings on the river begin with the smell of wood smoke hanging in a cool breeze, meadowlarks singing from sage-lined hillsides, and a rosy hue in the eastern sky? That's part of it; but unrequited love requires an element of lust if it's to last. It's feeling the power of a springer on the end of my line that makes me come back for more. When my instincts elevate, adrenaline spikes and endorphins kick in. Like the morning a salmon grabbed my rig and took off with me in hot pursuit. "It must be a big one. Take your time. Your drag is set just right," a watchful angler coached.

The salmon eventually tired and was swept over the falls, where it rode swells and battled cross-eddies until led to the net. That would have been a good ending, but there was more. I returned to my position in the line-up and two casts later felt a three-part throb, followed by a for-sure pull-down of another salmon. I set the hook. "Fish on!"

To celebrate my two-fish day, I drove to the nearest convenience store and returned with a six-pack to share with the congenial netter and his fishing buddy. "A beer for each net job," I said, handing them each a cold one.

It was the kind of day that leads to habit.

Float planes ready for take-off on a dock at Ketchikan, Alaska.

Part 2. Far-Flung Adventures

Take a giant step outside your mind.
—Gerry Goffin

one more LAST CAST

HURRICANES, DORADO, AND BAR SOAP

SIX WEEKS BEFORE A planned fishing trip to the Sea of Cortez, I Googled "Baja" to find headlines that read, "Hunger, Looting and Violence Follow Hurricane Odile's Path Across Baja California." Needless to say, I didn't share the news with Nancy.

Whether whimsy or seeking relief from seasonal affective disorder, my long-time friend Ted had bought three tickets at the Tri-Cities January Sportsmen Show for a four-night, three-day fishing adventure out of La Paz. "If you guys can't go," he told Ken and me, "I'll find somebody else. We've got a year to figure it out."

I recalled another friend who'd traveled to Baja once a year to camp on white-sand beaches, drink ice-cold *cerveza* for cheap, and catch exotic fish. While the scene attracted, I never took him up on offers to go along. *Maybe this was my chance,* I thought. Armed with a brochure that Ted brought back from the Baja Pirates' booth, I spent four months trying to convince Nancy that I should go. Admittedly, her misgivings related to an earlier business trip to Mexico. Something to do with a night of rum and Coke at the wrong end of Villahermosa followed by a pick-pocketed wallet. "You're going to go regardless of what I say," she finally said, after which I immediately phoned Ted to let him know I had the green light.

Ted, in hock for $2,700 worth of trip vouchers, turned up the heat in late July. E-mails went back and forth while we sorted out our busy retiree schedules. I was reminded that planning trips with two other guys is like having a second child. Things become complicated in an exponential rather than an additive way. What little ill feeling remained after I vetoed their September plans due to my desire to fish the fall Chinook salmon season was forgiven when Hurricane Odile, a Category 3 storm, devastated Los Cabos on September 17, leaving thousands of people without water and electricity.

Fast-forward to six weeks after the big storm. We managed to rebook a flight and secure an arrival date for late October. The Sea of Cortez from 29,000 feet was spectacular: wide, sandy beaches, deep valleys, arroyos split by broad rios, sweeping headlands. All mirrored against a backdrop of cumulus clouds suspended over a big, blue sea. But it wasn't all mental bliss and beautiful scenery. I woke up the morning of departure with a raving sinus infection. My nose was scraped sore from constant wiping with industrial-grade paper towels I pilfered from the airplane restroom, and my eardrums felt like they would burst on descent. Regardless, I tried to maintain levity. "Don't mess up your immigration form," I told Ken. "If you do, they'll throw you in jail and there's nothing Ted and I can do other than inform Sue when we return home without you."

It wasn't until we reached the crowded terminal that Ted shared, "I was told someone would meet us at the airport."

I recalled another business trip where a non-sanctioned taxi driver approached me at the Mexico City luggage return only to be arrested by *policios* before we made it out of the main terminal. Then there was the time I got into a two-tone VW bug that wasn't a taxi. Those experiences had made me wary of south-of-the-border limousine service

Sometimes relying on faith gets you where you need to go. Other times it bites you in the butt. The book was still out on this one because we opted not to rent a car. But as luck would have it, the shuttle driver for Baja Pirates recognized the searching look of three gringo anglers, grabbed our bags with a, "Welcome to Cabo, *mi amigos*," and we were safely on our way.

Following a brief introduction, Raul asked, "What hotel are you staying at?"

"We don't know," Ted replied. "We thought we were staying with you."

Several cell phone calls later, Raul figured it out. "You'll be staying at the Hotel Marina, where the Baja Pirates' office is."

That's when Ken asked, "What kind of rooms do we have?

"Separate, I think," Ted replied.

The two-hour drive north took us past small towns with 30-kilometer-per-hour speed bumps, cloud-shrouded hills, harbors peppered with fishing boats, tiny roadside memorials and concrete block shacks. Signs of devastation were everywhere. The most interesting example was a roadside McDonald's stand, golden arches torn off by hurricane winds. Still working off the two-pack of crackers provided by complacent flight attendants on the flight from San Francisco, we talked Raul into pulling over at a roadside café for *bisteak* and *empanadas* washed down with ice-cold Pacifico. Ten dollars US apiece covered the deal.

La Paz was not the sleepy little Mexican village I imagined.

At population 350,000, the southern entrance was a mix of industrial and broken-down shacks along a four-lane highway. Reserve water containers graced the top of nearly every flat-topped building. Business establishments had barred windows and doors. A large number of houses appeared abandoned. As Raul explained, "Still working on it so they don't have to pay taxes."

Local color included an elderly man on crutches begging at the first traffic signal. "He's fake," Raul said. "Local people know."

Hotel Marina was located at the terminus of an attractive ocean-side promenade and fronted by a large boat basin. As one pot-bellied retiree later shared, "A harbor where boat dreams come to die."

The hotel boasted of 89 *habitaciones*, a spa, and full-service restaurant. Separate rooms, however, turned out to be a three twin-bed suite with a view of the parking lot and decor that included suspicious burn marks above the only electrical outlet. No more than six other rooms were occupied due to "concern over the hurricane."

After we unpacked and bed selections were made, it was to the poolside bar for happy hour. *Hey, we were in Mexico and would soon be fishing!* I washed down a 500-mg Tylenol with Codeine #3 with an ice-cold Pacifico, followed by a *grande* margarita. Call it overkill or call it self-medication in time of need. Ted and Ken did likewise, except for the Tylenol. Our total bar tab was a modest $15, which proved you don't have to follow a lineup of geriatrics to find a bargain in La Paz. Despite harboring a life-long fantasy that involved watching a south-of-the-border stripper launch ping-pong balls from her vagina, I retired to my twin bed with the sun still above the horizon. Ted and Ken opted to walk the promenade.

A feverish sinusitis slumber led to a codeine-induced hallucination of an indescribable nature. Although Ted's cell phone alarm failed, the loud chirping of sparrows on the lanai served as an effective wake-up call. Hotel vouchers were redeemed for breakfast, after which we were shuttled to a small harbor that held the Baja Pirate fleet. As our assigned guide, Jesus (that would be hey-zoos, not gee-zus) explained, "First we catch sardines for bait."

After an hour of jigging a six-foot-long string of Mylar-tipped flies in the main La Paz harbor, I was reminded of playing the scales before a recital; a pianists version of foreplay. Sometimes you have to warm to the task before approaching the main event. In our case, small fish had to be caught before we could catch big fish. The hills were shrouded in a smoky haze and the warm salt air smelled of petroleum byproducts. An hour-and-a-half cruise down a scenic coastline in a 21-foot open Panga followed.

The technique was to flat-line live sardines in near shore waters ranging from 20 to 200 feet deep. Medium-weight 7-foot Ugly Sticks proved sensitive enough to detect when our bait sardine was getting chased. Action started fast and furious, but hooksets were infrequent. "Needlefish," Jesus explained. "They steal your bait."

When Jesus thumped one needlefish on the head with the butt of his gaff and hacked the lower jaw off another before releasing them, I was reminded of anglers who throw suckers on the bank and cut the fins off dogfish sharks. As if this would make a difference.

The only rainbow-hued dorado of the day swallowed my bait sardine while I spooled off a bird's nest created by casting directly into a southwest breeze. Meanwhile, Ted and Ken reeled in a trio of *sierras,* or Spanish mackerel, and a trumpet fish. When the sardine supply was depleted, Jesus brought out the big rods and we trolled skirted jigs for marlin. Frigate birds circled over the sea like buzzards over roadkill. Dead puffer fish and rafts of butterflies dominated latent storm debris. The sound of a big reel screaming for attention alerted me from a sleep-deprived nod-off, but the sailfish was gone before I could get the rod out of the holder. Two hours of mindless trolling later, we were reminded to catch more sardines the next day and deny interest in billfish.

The important part was acquiring our sea legs and landing several fish, none of which we had experienced on the end of a line before. Sometimes different gets a prize. The small dorado was turned over to the hotel chef, who paired it with *frijoles, tortillas, ensalada verde,* and guacamole. Presentation and flavor were more than adequate to keep him from getting "chopped." The rest of the evening's entertainment involved relaxing on the deck and watching the setting sun drop over the Sea of Cortez.

Day two was more of the same: trade vouchers for a custom-order breakfast, shuttle to the boat harbor, jig for bait, experience a scenic boat ride along the coastline, fast-troll sardines behind the boat, catch exotic fish. Ted and Ken each caught a nice dorado, while I honed a technique that kept my interest and enticed strikes from bottom fish. After watching Ken and Ted repeatedly get tangled, I let my line out several yards past where their sardines swam. When I felt the frantic pulse of my bait sardine, I let out more line. Three play-outs produced my first grab. But rather than run or jump, the fish dove straight for the bottom. This behavior created a challenge because Jesus, with dorado on his mind, kept trolling at a steady clip. Barely showing interest, he reached for my star drag and tightened it until the 30-pound mono leader snapped at the swivel.

I knew what it felt like to bring up a barn-door halibut from the depths of the Pacific Ocean and I'd seen pictures of giant grouper. Put those two thoughts together in a tropical setting and all I could think was that Jesus had just broken off the largest and most exotic fish of my life. Sensing my angst, he slowed the boat after my next hookset. It was all I could do to gain line while the fish fought like a bowling ball. I'd never felt such dead weight on the end of my line. "Pargo," Jesus said when he gaffed a chunky, copper-striped fish that weighed no more than 15 pounds. "Don't grab it by the lip."

One look at a mouth full of razor-sharp teeth and its spiny dorsal fin and I let Jesus remove the hook. Using my "let out more line" technique, I hooked and landed two more pargo while Ted and Ken wondered what I knew that they didn't. The day was capped off by casting to actively feeding barracuda and *sierra* that worked over a school of frantic baitfish within view of the harbor.

Arriving back at the dock, we were assailed by an excited woman tourist with a story about a 20-foot-long sailfish that interrupted her fourth vodka Collins of the morning. "Maybe not quite that long," she replied, after I pointed out a rusted-out Suburban in the parking lot as reference.

"I've been coming here for seven years and never caught a sailfish," her husband said with more than a little chagrin. "First time we bring the women, they get one."

Fishing teaches you something about close friends. In our case, we each had equal enthusiasm and tolerance for the sport. There were no spats or whining, and individual highlights were eagerly shared. But there's more that you learn when you sleep three to a room. For example, who gets up in the middle of the night to pee. Unusual sleeping attire. Who needs a night-light.

Pillow arrangement. The odd noise in the night that includes throat-clearing, burping, huffing, moaning, shouting, and snoring. Unfortunately, any insight gained regarding such behavior is generally not novel.

Perhaps the most enlightening moment of the trip transpired when I came out of our bathroom holding a complimentary bar of soap that had been reduced to the size of a postage stamp after less than a handful of showers. "This hotel provides the smallest bar of soap I've ever seen," I said. "If you're not careful it could get lost in a crease."

"Too much information," Ken replied.

Not to be dissuaded, I told Ken about the coffee can filled with soap slivers in my younger sister's shower stall. "I don't have a clue what she does with them," I said.

Ken had a ready answer. "I save the slivers and smash them into a new bar. It's wasteful to throw them away."

"Probably saves three cents," I replied, after admitting I threw old soap slivers away. "What if it's a different brand?"

"It's not an issue because I always buy Ivory or Dial."

Upon further reflection, I couldn't help think that a little sliver of soap could be like starter sourdough. It would keep giving as long as you took care of it and didn't screw with the original recipe.

Our last day on the water produced a nice pargo and a cabrilla for Ted and Ken, respectively. I took partial credit for their success after sharing my "let out slack when you sense a frantic sardine" technique over breakfast. Meanwhile, I contented myself hooking needlefish, including an acrobatic four-footer that fought with the strength and agility of a marlin. There were empty moments for sure, like on any quest for trophy fish in foreign waters, but spectacular geology surrounded by azure water entertained like big-screen TV.

The highlight of the day took place when Jesus grabbed a rod, slung a sardine to the flash of a feeding dorado, set the hook, and handed the rod back to Ken, who expertly brought the fish to the boat.

We made one last stop to troll along a small rock island covered with waist-high piles of bird crap. That's where Ted accidentally caught a booby who tried to steal his bait sardine, and I hooked and landed two dorado in less than a half-hour. It was a "two down in the bottom of the ninth" moment that salvaged my day. I'd heard stories of the fighting prowess of dorado and they did not disappoint: socket-jarring takes, long, slashing runs, acrobatic leaps. Too pretty to kill, really.

It's interesting how things wind down. Rather than revisit trip highlights, breakfast conversation on the morning of departure degenerated into discussion of lower GI tracts. Ted shared that he'd got out of sync the first day. "I didn't take a dump so I had to take two the second day. But I'm back to normal. All it takes is one cup of coffee and I'm ready to go."

Ken was quick to reply that he was not so regular. "I had to get up at midnight again last night. Must be those lunch burritos."

Not wanting to be left out of the conversation, I added, "I need to go twice a day or I'm out of sorts. Think of it as an a.m. and a p.m. B. M."

"Too much information," Ken said.

Leaving La Paz on the Day of the Dead, Raul chauffeured us via the Pacific Coast Highway so we could visit the legendary Hotel California in Todos Santos and purchase over-priced jewelry and tequila from merchants who were desperate for tourist trade. According to all reports, fishing was slow. Hurricane winds had scattered baitfish and the toothy predators that ate them. Still, we managed to add ten species to our life list. Fishing trips that take you thousands of miles from home waters tend to broaden the angling experience.

More inner ear pain during take-off and landing due to mucus-clogged sinus passages, a token package of in-flight crackers refused and two airport bars later, we arrived home safe and sound. After five days on the road, it was almost as if Baja never happened. Wife greets at the airport, unpack bag, toss dirty underwear in the laundry, share selected trip highlights, settle into old routine.

Soon upon return, however, I found opportunity to try Ken's recycling trick with a bar of personal soap that had been worn down to a nub. It was evident that we (i.e., me and the bar of soap) had been together a long time. You could even say that our relationship had been intimate. There's more to making the transfer than you might think though. Both the recipient bar of soap and the sliver must be malleable. In my case, the distinctive concave shape of Irish Spring also came into play. The primary decision point, however, revolved around the amount of suds left in the sliver versus the potential of losing it in a crease.

Once the joining of old onto new was complete, I admit to a special attraction of watching the two pieces of soap meld into one. Tracking incorporation was less of an obsession than a focused activity in a setting where the mind usually roams free. Whether an analytical exercise or excuse to stand in the shower after sinuses were drained and body parts that do not normally see the light of day were scrubbed, the process diverted from adulation of my member.

Several days later, maybe a week (I didn't keep track), the old sliver of soap disappeared like some kind of pipe dream. I gave the newish bar of Irish Spring the blind man's test, that is, strolled my fingers over its surface with my eyes closed, but the transformation was complete. Like a once-in-a-lifetime fishing trip to the Baja de Sur, the tiny sliver of recycled soap was gone, but not forgotten.

one more LAST CAST

SHE-BOY-GUN

MY VERY FIRST and only fishing adventure on the Great Lakes morphed from a golfing vacation with brother Daran. "I have guaranteed tee times for all the best courses near Kohler, including Whistling Straits, site of the PGA Championship," he said. "It will be just you, me, and my two assistants."

While a week of golf seemed like a good idea, as our September departure date closed in, I couldn't ignore the fact that I would miss the peak of the fall Chinook salmon run to the Hanford Reach. Nevertheless, I signed up for the trip. Sometimes you have to trust your older brother.

Our first evening in Sheboygan (pronounced "She-Boy-Gun") found us at the waterfront looking for a place to eat. This was my second introduction to an American city whose name is easily screwed up by West Coast tourists, the first one being Gloucester (pronounced "Glau-ster"), which made me wonder how three-syllable names become two and phonics can be ignored. A flotilla of charter and pleasure boats lined the harbor with enthusiastic groups of anglers standing by their catch for hero photos. The raucous squawk of circling gulls and colorful kites flying in the breeze completed the scene. It could have been the Oregon Coast except for lack of salt air. When I walked into a bait-and-tackle shop for a fishing report, the clerk said, "It's good for Kings, with some steelhead and lake trout being taken."

Figuring that hanging around the bait shop for 10 minutes was about as close as I was going to get to fish that weren't fried golden brown and surrounded by French fries, I left with a handful of brochures.

As luck would have it, a wrench was thrown into golfing plans when our grand finale, the Jack Nicklaus "Golden Bear" course, was found to be under repair. After experiencing four of Wisconsin's finest links in three days, my golfing buddies were not willing to settle for a second-tier experience. While we fretted the situation at a crowded Hooter's bar in Green Bay, I planted the seed to go fishing.

"Check this out," I said, holding up a brochure I'd grabbed the first night. "We can buy a 5-hour trip on a charter boat for $320. That's only $80 apiece. I paid twice that for the last two rounds of golf. Not to mention all the money you pros won from me playing skins."

Several glasses of Milwaukee's Best, a pile of grilled brats and two hours of cleavage later, they warmed to the idea, so I called to reserve a trip. Nobody wanted to get up at 4:00 a.m., and the idea of three-hour twilight trip seemed too short, so we settled on a noon to 5:00 p.m. outing.

The next morning arrived quickly. We ate a big breakfast, paying 1960s prices for ham and eggs at the 8th Street Diner in downtown Sheboygan. Afterwards, we visited a convenience store to purchase drinks and snacks for the boat ride. It was a blue sky, T-shirt day with a slight breeze blowing from the southwest. Non-resident daily licenses were purchased before we lolled nervously near our vessel, the 35-foot *Sea Dog*, and watched the morning crowd come in. Every boat had fish. One group had 27, ranging from 2 to 17 pounds and consisting of a mix of steelhead, salmon, and lake trout. Catch was hung on the board outside the bait shop, pictures were taken, and tips were exchanged.

We were pumped. Fishing looked hot. But at 10 minutes before the scheduled departure, where was our captain and crew? Several boats were tethered to the dock with motors on idle and rods in holders, but our craft was as still as a morgue. While we nervously waited for someone to show, the adjacent boat captain walked by and jibed, "Doesn't look like the ol' *Sea Dog* is eager to take you fishing."

About then I decided to take one last run to the public restroom. While I contemplated my navel at the urinal, a curled-haired man wearing baggy blue jeans and a ragged T-shirt bolted from the toilet stall without pausing at the sink. Guess who was at the helm of the *Sea Dog* when I returned to the slip? You guessed it: the man who did not wash his hands after he went number two. The good news was, he was not the bait boy.

At noon sharp, twin diesels were fired up, the deckhand arrived, and we were invited on board. We pulled away from the slip and exited a 100-yard-wide harbor framed by corrugated steel walls. Multicolored flags from tall boat masts flapped in the breeze. Bank anglers lined the edge out to the north pier. What was a light chop in the harbor built to large rollers as we motored offshore. *Was it possible to get seasick on a lake?* I wondered.

The fishing arrangement begs for explanation. Six downriggers with 12-pound lead balls were lined up across the aft, starting from the starboard side. Two rods were deployed off outriggers and two off the back using "dipsy doodles." Our arsenal also included a large wooden side-planer shaped like a half-pallet that positioned lures 30 yards or so from the port side. Each line was attached in sequence to the main line with a rubber band and positioned to keep lines spread apart. The longest lines were spooled out over 50 yards. With the exception of outrigger rod holders mounted on top of the cab, we had full view of ten rods off the back of the boat. The end result of this complicated setup was fourteen lines in the water. According to the captain, we could have employed eighteen rods or three apiece, if you counted the crew. Needless to say, the lineup required constant attention.

Hung by treble hooks on a four-foot-wide sheet of faded plywood were several dozen 4-inch spoons of assorted colors. Our deckhand (also second mate and bait boy) tied on several different ones, including his favorite, tiger-striped orange and black. "I'll swap them out after we see which ones catch fish," he said.

Rod #4, on a downrigger line, was the first to twitch. Our deckhand was quick to grab the rod but the fish got off before he could set the hook. "Probably about a half-pound," he said.

My designated rod was the first to achieve a good hookset. The fish came to the surface and took several yards of line before I wrenched the rod from its holder. One slashing run and two jumps later I worked it to the net, after which high fives were exchanged all around. Its silver flanks shone bright with a tinge of gray above the lateral line. Upon close examination, the characteristic square tail of a steelhead was revealed. "Skamania stock," our deckhand said.

"Transplanted from our home state," I replied, trying for partial credit.

Waves reached four-foot swells by the time I hooked my second fish, which made footing difficult. I got knocked to my knees but kept reeling until it was safely netted. This one was declared a lake trout based on its spotting pattern. Looking green behind the gills, Daran made a brief cameo appearance to fight a fish while I held onto his belt, but he returned to the comfort of the cabin for the duration of the day.

The rest of us alternated turns at the rods over the next few hours to ensure willing participants had an equal chance. The end result was one double, several takedowns missed, and one fish lost at the net due to lazy reeling. Our grand total was an 11-fish mix of Chinook, coho, steelhead, and lake trout, ranging from 3 to 14 pounds. When first removed from the water, the fish appeared nearly identical. Only after the platinum finish faded was their true heritage revealed.

Nobody argued for "one last cast" when 4:30 p.m. rolled around. After being slammed by waves most of the afternoon, we were ready for dry land. Fish were unloaded at the dock for a group picture, an 80-gallon cooler was purchased, and our catch was iced down. Unfortunately, we arrived at the airport to find that our precious cargo was required to be shipped on either blue or dry ice, neither of which could be found before takeoff. So we dumped a pile of crushed ice on the terminal sidewalk and hoped that the hold of a wide-body Boeing 777 at 30,000 feet was kept as cold as a refrigerator. What we also hadn't counted on was that Great Lakes salmon have white flesh due to a predominantly fish diet. Consequently, their flavor resembled canned cat food, which reinforced that you should never leave salmon at home to catch salmon on the road.

one more LAST CAST

EIGHT SECONDS

THERE'S A WILD opening scene in the 1948 John Huston-directed cinema classic, *Treasure of the Sierra Madre* where a gang of Mexican bandits on horseback attempt to rob a fast-moving train. Bullets fly between the marauders and a handful of train passengers trying to hold them off. After the gang is defeated and rides off, Humphrey Bogart's character brags, "How many did you get? I got me three of them. Credit me with three!"

My first guided trip for albacore out of Westport, Washington, included much of the same bravado. There was no wasted night at a No-Tell Motel where your brain screams for sleep when the alarm goes off at 2:00 a.m. With five pairs of berths on the 50-foot *Hula Girl*, ten of us boarded in late evening with sleeping bags and provisions for the next day of fishing. There were challenges to a good night's sleep, for sure, such as aberrant vocalization, random bunkmates who sat on your head, and the irregular drone of the below-deck head. However, for the most part we slept soundly, lulled by the tympanic hum of twin screw John Deeres while the *Hula Girl* cruised down the Washington coast at a steady 16 knots. Then again, excess diesel fumes may have been involved.

Skies were still pitch-black when we staggered up from our below-deck berths to watch Captain Steve demonstrate how to cast a live anchovy using a medium-heavy Ugly Stick and Penn 340GT level-wind. That's when a tuna snuck up in the dark to eat the fish that dangled on the end of his line. Steve yelled, "Get out the bait rods!" and we responded like buck privates on day one of boot camp to free-spool live anchovies into the pre-dawn void.

Opportunity to be full of it began before the first bite cooled. "I got two out of that school."

"That big one is mine."

"I hooked one every time I put out a bait."

In other words, if you had it, you showed it. It was a day when the number of fish brought to the gaff was a measure of your manhood. I know my chest swelled with every successful hook-up. Conversely, if you want to know what lonely is, be the only guy on the boat without an albacore on the end of your line.

The technique was not complicated. We cruised warm surface waters until we located a school of feeding tuna. You lob casted a live anchovy into the melee and free-spooled line from your Penn 340GT until a hungry albacore grabbed the bait. Captain Steve instructed us to be patient. "Let the fish run for at least eight seconds before you lock down your bail."

But like one eager angler said when Steve turned his back, "Yeah! One, two, three, eight!"

Albacore are built for speed. Following the initial grab, there were two main stages to the fight. Action began with a long, searing run. During this stage, all you could do was hold on and hope the drag was set correctly. Once the albacore slowed, a slugfest began. During stage two, albacore swim in a wide arc with their head pointed down. They don't give an inch without taking it back on the next swing of the arc. Your only recourse is to hold onto the deck rail and pump and reel, pump and reel, pump and reel. Just when you think your arms will fall off, there will be a flash of silver and blue—your signal to yell, "Color!"—and a deck hand will come running with a long-handled gaff.

There was no rest for the weary once the bite was on. Twice we had on eight fish at once, a situation that led to crossed lines and lost fish. However, the scream of a drag or the sight of a bloody tuna flopping at your feet made you forget your misfortune and go for another bait. The exception was two geriatric anglers who remained content to let the rest of us do the catching while they rested in the main cabin. Only on congenial charter boats does old age have benefits that extend beyond Medicare, senior discounts, and rest home living.

Captain Steve did not team up with a spotter plane to locate schools of tuna. A course was charted until deck hands saw excited baitfish, porpoises, or dive-bombing birds. Absent these clues, we trolled skirted jigs behind the boat until a tuna struck, after which Captain Steve shut the engine off and spurred us to our bait rods. Little encouragement was required.

Like most fishing scenarios, presentation was everything. Once, while examining my line for weak spots, Captain Steve noticed that my bait anchovy was hooked deep in the top of its head. "Who baited you?" he yelled in the general direction of a deck hand.

"I did," I admitted, rather sheepishly.

I eventually got it right. The correct way to tether a live anchovy is to hook it behind the upper collar of the operculum or gill cover, barely into their head tissue. This detail is important. Anchovies hooked in this manner swim freely into the strike zone. Anchovies hooked too deep will bleed out and swim at the surface. Having active live bait is critical in order to get a tuna's attention. Lethargic anchovies do not result in hooksets.

By early afternoon, we'd filled up two 300-gallon fish boxes and every other storage container that could be iced down. The total catch—174 albacore for eight relentless and two passive fishermen—was split ten ways after gifting 24 fish to the captain and crew. No matter how you count it, that's a lot of tuna noodle casserole.

Besides bringing home more tuna than we could eat, there were other highlights to the trip: sunrise over the ocean, sea-birds, dolphins, ocean sunfish, blue sharks, and shared theory on why bananas produce bad karma. There was also memorable nightlife by the wharf. Who could forget the local karaoke line-up and other *Star Search* hopefuls who entertained at Cowboy Bob's Bar and Grill until it was time for us to shove off?

As for my total, credit me with 19 albacore. How many did you get?

109 Steps

"One more hole in your gut and you'll have a golf course," Leroy said when I shared news of a recent hernia operation. I must mention that Leroy's idea of golf is whacking the ball around a 9-hole pitch-and-putt.

"I'm already there if you count my belly button," I replied.

The first five holes were the result of a prostatectomy, the robot-assisted da Vinci version of surgery, to be exact. Blame those holes on me being the one guy out of six who gets diagnosed with prostate cancer. The hernia operation added three more holes. Blame that trio of scars on an Alaskan fishing trip that involved 109 steps.

The Alaska trip started off smoothly. We arrived in Ketchikan, where an eight-passenger de Havilland DMC-3 Otter warmed up for boarding at dockside. The reality of a fishing trip to the land of the midnight sun began to sink in when we saw anglers unload boxes of fish for transport home. On the short flight over Clarence Strait to Prince of Wales Island, we passed over tree-shrouded islands, low-lying wisps of clouds, and a giant cruise ship that pushed waves.

"Welcome to Thorne Bay," our host Paul said when he greeted us at the floatplane dock. After piling gear into his rusty '87 Suburban, we headed to the only grocery store within 50 miles, where we piled a shopping cart high with cold cereal, summer sausage, bacon, eggs, pancake mix, syrup, cookies, chips, bread, cheese, lunchmeat, more chips, peanut butter, jam, ground coffee, milk, yogurt, orange juice, paper towels, and Saran wrap. The next stop was the liquor store for two cases of beer and a half-gallon of Jim Beam.

Sixty miles of back roads, one bear sighting and two hours of drizzle later, we arrived at Flyquest, a "do it yourself" lodge in Whale's Pass that catered to anglers on a budget. For $165 a day you got a bed with linen, use of a 14-foot runabout with a 15-horsepower outboard, and were fed a three-course dinner if you showed up at the host's dining room table by 6:00 p.m. The lodge consisted of three rustic cabins. Ours contained four single beds, a small kitchenette and a bathroom. Plywood floors were painted stone gray, walls were unstained OSB and cabinetry was rough-cut pine. Your catch was stored in two deep freezers that rested on the front porch.

Eleven flights of wooden stairs led from our cabin down to the spacious three-bedroom home of our hosts near the water. Three-tab asphalt shingles nailed to a grand total of 109 steps provided traction. A rocky beach with a covered fish-cleaning station and four tethered skiffs completed the scene. One trip down the steep staircase was all it took to reinforce the notion that you should bring everything needed for the day's fishing the first time around.

Our experience began with an evening of a thousand casts that culminated in a single coho salmon apiece. "The rain put them down," Paul said, in an admirable attempt to shore up our darkened moods.

The truth was, no one except Paul had a clue what to do that first night other than toss spinners in all directions of the compass. Lacking a depth finder in our small crafts, cueing off bottom features was impossible. And, in our haste to get on the water, nobody had consulted a tide table. You might say we had not yet acquired a sense of place. Battling no-see-ums was also a deterrent. "Biting little bastards," we joked, but the only thing humorous was Leroy in his protective head net. "Good luck picking up chicks in that outfit," Bob said.

Rain let up overnight to reveal dark clouds that hinted of open sky. "The trip is all about killing coho," Paul had said when the trip was planned four months earlier over a pitcher of Irish Death. And with a six-fish limit, we were anxious enough to kill coho to get on the water at the crack of dawn. Paul and I experimented casting from the boat with Wiggle Warts, Mepps, and tube jigs, while Andy and Bob stuck with silver-and-chartreuse Vibrax spinners.

It turned out that hooking coho was easy. Catching them was not. Of the first six coho I hooked, four got off before the net came out. When the bay calmed, a constant parade of salmon could be seen cruising towards the entrance of Fish Creek. Large schools produced impressive open water V-waves. Small pods dimpled and splashed along the shoreline. For every fish that rolled, ten more swam beneath. I finished off my six-fish limit after dinner while Bob and Andy worked the creek channel. A day spent catching coho, along with increased numbers returning to

Fish Creek, had improved our acumen several-fold.

But it wasn't all pleasure in the wilderness. For starters, four guys sleeping an arm's length away defines close quarters. It took exactly one day to find that whatever politeness exists among friends deteriorates when you get comfortable with your surroundings. Rather than let things get completely out of control, I laid down the law regarding bathroom etiquette. "Either shut the door, use odor elimination spray, or turn on the fan," I said to Leroy over a bowl of Raisin Bran. "You were zero for three."

Half a dozen boats worked the bay the second morning, but with over a mile of shoreline available, competition was not an issue. The tide retreated to expose fish rolling and splashing in nearly every shoreline embayment and along scattered kelp beds. I caught two coho in successive casts on a Wiggle Wart before switching to a rainbow-colored #4 Mepps spinner to finish out my limit. After Bob boated his limit, we practiced catch and release until it was time for bacon and eggs. Coho acrobatics in effect included twists, flips, back flops, spins, rolls, headshakes, and broad jumps. I witnessed three fish jumping in unison, like trained dolphins after a beach ball. One enthusiastic coho took a header against the side of our boat.

Fishing can take its toll on even the most devoted angler, however. During a group nap that followed the second day of fishing, Paul snored so loudly I had to move to the front porch and lay on the ground. Meanwhile, Bob napped soundly with the aid of earplugs. Leroy gave up on the idea of rest and took a walk.

I dedicated one evening at Whales Pass to fly fishing from the bank with my 7-weight Cortland. The fourth selection from my fly box, a pink Marabou streamer, produced a pickup, after which I lost three different coho three different ways. The first fish picked up the fly but came off early. The second one stayed on until I thought I might land it. After a powerful run that took it halfway to the other side of the bay, it swam back and forth, parallel to the shore, until the hook pulled free. Warming to the task, I fought my third fish with more patience. Unfortunately, it made one last run straight towards me. I struggled to get out of the way but it swam between my legs with the precision of a heat-seeking missile and broke off.

Teamed with Leroy on day four, I caught my largest coho, maybe 12 pounds, before our kicker motor died. Paddling a single spare oar against the tide proved futile, so we put ashore and flipped a coin to see who would walk back to the lodge for a tow. I lost the toss but met up with a local on a four-wheeler and bummed a lift. I offered him $5 for his trouble when we got to the lodge, but he opted for a beer with Bob and Paul instead. By the time Leroy and I returned with the disabled boat, my four-wheeler friend was surrounded by a pile of empties.

Their merriment had attracted two young ladies from an adjacent cabin, both of whom disclosed a Christian affiliation between long pulls on their Budweisers. One woman had "Glory" tattooed on her right shoulder, a diamond stud in her nose, and a suspicious bulge between her lower lip and gums. The other wore a Boston Red Sox ball cap, mirror sunglasses, and a hot-pink t-shirt that showcased more cleavage than prudent in mosquito country. It turned out they were regular visitors to Whales Pass and harvested coho by snagging, a practice allowed in the tidal zone. When I asked in jest, "Do you have a special technique?" they set their beers down to demonstrate a series of exaggerated jerking motions. I couldn't help wonder what kind of ride was given on their busload of faith.

Leroy and I spent the remainder of the afternoon casting to large schools of coho that split off like a flock of geese when they approached. After Leroy tagged out, I fly fished off the back of the boat. He amused himself catching tiny staghorn sculpin with a pink jig.

What happened next was my Waterloo. That evening, after T-bone steak and apple pie, our hosts requested we help move a disabled refrigerator to the main parking area above the lower cabins. The undertaking started out okay. Four of us ganged up to move the dated appliance, but with limited space to operate, Bob and I had to take over to finish the job. By the time we reached the top staircase, my back was shot. A handful of Ibuprofen and a good night's rest provided an illusion of recovery.

We hit the road the next morning with over 300 pounds of frozen coho fillets in the back of Paul's Suburban. Fish boxes were transferred at the floatplane dock and we were soon on our way home. It wasn't until disembarking at Ketchikan led to a sharp searing pain in my groin that I sensed something was wrong.

Luckily, I came prepared. After taking my aisle seat on the flight to Seattle, I self-medicated with a pair of Tylenol #3s. Once the codeine kicked in, I engaged a wide-eyed toddler who initiated conversation by holding up two fingers. "So, two years old, eh? Are you a big girl now?" I asked.

"Yes."

"What makes you a big girl?"

She was silent.

"Do you help Mommy in the kitchen?

More silence.

"Do you take care of your dollies?"

No response.

"Is it because you are taller now than when you were a baby?"

The last question struck a chord. The little tyke twirled in her seat, cocked her head sideways and held both hands high over her head. "Jamie is this big," she said.

So much for priding yourself on the ability to communicate with small children.

Upon arriving home, the situation called for careful monitoring, a relatively simple task if you soap your privates in the shower. Analyzing the marble-sized bulge in my abdominal fascia detracted from adulation of my member, but in a non-schizophrenic way. I was reminded of a friend who'd experienced a hernia in high school. His first thought was that he had acquired an extra testicle from too frequent masturbation. (The key phrase here being "too frequent.") In my case, medical diagnosis revealed what I had suspected since the awkward stroll up the loading ramp in Ketchikan: I had a hernia.

Convalescence was not in the cards, however. Two days later, brother Dusty called to see if I wanted to fish the Walla Walla River. "I have a hernia," I shared, "but I think I can make it up the trail."

The two-hour hike up the South Fork trail was tolerable, but debilitating pain nearly paralyzed me when I attempted to ford the river in thigh-high current. To make matters worse, Dusty had a bad knee and needed help getting across. "My leg strength is about 15 percent gone," he said.

"More like 50 percent," I muttered after watching him stumble along the bank.

I sat down only to experience a feeling of electricity that shot from my knees up my spine. *Things are getting worse,* I thought, *Dusty is going to have to build a raft and float me back down the river.* Not until I looked down did I notice that I was being attacked by a swarm of harvester ants whose nest I chose to sit on. The rest of the day went without major mishap.

I even caught a trout or two.

Complicating timely surgical repair of my hernia was a commitment to attend a scientific review on the proposed Pebble Mine project back in Alaska. Meanwhile, I'd been popping over-the-counter painkillers for five days straight. Unable to perform the simplest chore, I felt like a bird with clipped wings. My hernia, exacerbated after the hike up the South Fork and two -days of chasing crawdads with grandkids at our cabin, had manifested itself into a bulge the size of a silver dollar.

It's interesting how the mind works. After flying to Anchorage and listening to three days of public testimony on the proposed Pebble Mine project, I was eager to go fishing again, regardless of the consequences. So I reserved a spot on a boat with a friend who migrated north to guide each summer. He promised that no hiking or heavy lifting would be involved.

The Kenai River flowed an intoxicating slate blue when I arrived at Bings Landing. It was early August, high noon, and the launch parking lot was almost empty. Although the peak of the sockeye salmon run had passed, I was eager to try my hand at "flossing." Imagine my surprise when I was handed a heavy-duty casting rod instead of a 9-weight fly rod. The fly, a token hank of red yarn knotted to a 4/0 hook, did not require a Renzetti Master vise to fabricate. The rod was not designed for playing a fish, rather to yank it to shore as quickly as possible, Alaska style. To get our presentation down to where sockeye swam, a two-ounce barrel sinker was affixed above 6 feet of 30-pound test monofilament leader.

As Bruce explained: "Toss the lead weight slightly upstream, about 15 feet out. Lower your rod tip until you feel the weight tick the bottom and let the fly swing across the current. When it slows, jerk!"

So that's what I did: sling, drift, swing, jerk. However, the level of pain during the first jerk was so severe that further efforts were limited to a version of the "sissy jerk." Meanwhile, a steady stream of lockjaw sockeye migrated past where I stood ankle-deep in swift current. Bruce's more refined flossing technique led to putting several salmon in the box, some hooked in the mouth and some in the "other mouth," as he described one foul-hooked specimen that he released.

"We would have landed 30 or 40 at the peak of the run," Bruce said. "But that was two weeks ago."

Only if "we" means you, I thought, reflecting on my inept technique.

I flew home that night and checked in to the hospital the next day. My only memory of surgery was a desire to go back to sleep after I woke from anesthesia, and that I got shoved out the swinging glass door with no love from the discharge nurse. The first night of recovery was spent in our spare bedroom wondering how guests managed a night's rest on such a cheap mattress. One thousand milligrams of Oxycodone, in combination with a summer lightning storm, led to dreams that involved all colors of the rainbow. Another word for the experience would be hallucination.

Day three post-surgery found me weak and dizzy, but on the road to mending. I downgraded my painkiller regimen to one Percocet per day and sought digestive relief with Dulcolax, oatmeal, and bananas. A pillow propped between my legs helped me rest in comfort. Day seven was noteworthy because it involved no prescription painkillers and the ability to put on socks. Ten days post-surgery found me fishing for salmon on the Columbia River and wishing I had purchased the power tilt option for my kicker motor. Loading gear bags and a cooler from the dock into my Hewescraft violated the surgeon's 15-pound lift limit but required taking a grand total of only two steps.

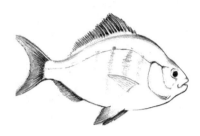

REDTAILS AND HIGH TIDE

IT WAS ONE HOUR BEFORE flood tide and the Pacific Ocean appeared angry. I glanced left at Eric when he leaned over to retrieve a pyramid sinker he had snagged on a barnacle-crusted ledge. It was Eric's first fishing trip to the Seal Rock area of the Oregon Coast and I wanted to get him and his friend Ed into a school of redtail surfperch. Concentrating on keeping a tight line when my mussel bait slid sideways in wicked crosscurrent, I heard a thunderous roar as a huge wave slammed against the base of the rock we stood on. I looked over to see if Eric's rain slicker was up to the task, but he disappeared in a wall of blue-green foam. When the giant wave subsided, the only evidence of Eric was of his spinning rod and reel laying cross-wise on the rock

On my God! Eric got washed off! My stomach churned and I fought a helpless feeling as I lowered my rod and peered into the crashing surf. There was no sign of a person, but where did Eric go? Looking behind to where seawater rushed from a deep, narrow crevasse, I saw his head and shoulders emerge like King Neptune rising from the deep. "Are you okay?" I yelled.

"My hand hurts," Eric mumbled, holding up his right wrist to show a four-inch jagged cut.

"Anything broken?"

"I don't think so, but my neck is sore."

Concerned that another big wave might also wash me off the rock, I searched for a handhold on the steep rock face made slick from wave splash. Meanwhile, surf pulsed and swirled around Eric's waist to remind us this wasn't a static system we were dealing with. "We've got to get you out of there in case another big wave hits," I said, reaching for Eric's outstretched hand. "Can you step up?"

Lacking solid footing, there was no way to lift his 240 pounds to safety without the aid of a block and tackle. My sense of urgency amplified when another sheet of spray shot high overhead. Only after an equally cautious Ed joined me could we manhandle a dazed and compliant Eric to safety.

What happened that day on Perch Rock was a revelation, what you could call improved understanding of the potential perils of the ocean. I had been pounded, pummeled, and pinned by waves while body surfing. I had felt the slam of chest-high waves over beach sand, climbed down sheer rock walls to re-cover fishing rigs, and chased the receding tide out to where cormorants roost. I had slipped and fallen into tide pools reaching for bait mussels. I had done all these things without serious mishap, and never once imagined getting washed off a rock by a giant wave.

What would it feel like to be knocked down by a wave having the force of a fire hose? I could only imagine: loss of equilibrium, light turns to dark, cold water crests your senses, the abrupt sting of salt water in your eyes and nose followed by a sharp pain in your neck. Only when dark turned to light and Eric saw blood oozing from a gash in his hand did he know it was not a bad dream. Only then did he recall standing on a rock, casting for redtails and that, out of nowhere, a big wave knocked him backwards into a narrow crevasse, submerging him, but not drowning him, for he had returned to the present, wet and cold and surrounded by crashing surf. And look! There is Dennis, yelling, "Are you okay?"

Eric's wife, Emily, arrived on the scene soon after sensing things had gone awry from her vantage point at the front window of their beach rental. While she consoled a subdued Eric, the sun broke through, as if to remind us that the ever-present shadow of death had passed.

As for Ed, when I asked if he still wanted to fish after Eric was hauled off to the emergency room in Newport, he replied, "Sure. That's what we came here for, wasn't it?"

Got to admire that in a guy.

In hindsight, it would have been nearly impossible to retrieve Eric if he had pitched forward into the crashing surf below. Divergent currents and jagged rocks prevented an effective approach to the surf zone. As for emergency equipment, we had none, and the nearest Coast Guard station was an hour away. Trying to snag him with spinning gear would not have done the trick. They don't drag for bodies with 12-pound test monofilament. By falling backwards, Eric ended up in the only place he could have been saved without being snookered by another wave like a sucker punch in a crowded bar.

The rogue wave was a "sneaker," a rare tidal event for sure, but one that occurred often enough to have a moniker. Indeed, one day before our fateful event, Oregon Public Broadcasting covered a memorial service at Smelt Sands State Park for two tourists who got washed out to sea while exploring a tide pool. I paused to read their flower-covered bronze plaque, more as a reminder of possibility than curiosity, before I walked out to my favorite rock to cast for greenling.

"Fifteen people got washed off rocks in Oregon last year," Nancy said when I returned to our condo in Yachats. "I read it on the back of the menu when we waited for our bowl of clam chowder at Mo's. I worry about you every time you go out there."

I couldn't count the number of times I had hauled in a stringer-full of surfperch from where Eric stood, oblivious to possibilities. What if I had moved left when Eric joined me instead of taking position to his right? Instinct towards self-preservation maybe, although a contributing factor to a day-gone-bad included inviting two rookies to fish in a situation where they had no clue. As an example, after arriving on the scene, Ed pointed to a rock where he planned to stand. "You might want to watch the next wave before you climb down," I said. "The tide is still coming in."

As if on cue, the next set of waves crashed high over the rock, submerging his exit lane. "I guess I'll stay up here," he replied.

Another way of summing up the debacle was my own naivety. I did not consider all the possibilities. I was like a babysitter with an impressive resume yet deficient when it came to responsibility.

I will return to Perch Rock for no other reason than the bite of a redtail elevates your senses. The distinct tap of their teeth and jaw on your bait keeps you in the game and makes you crave more. Admittedly, some bites are subtle—like the tick of a walleye, in which case you wonder, is it a crab? Most bites, however, impart the sharp tension of a pick drawn across a banjo string.

Because surfperch operate in turbulent flow, they don't attack your bait as much as they dodge and feint like Muhammad Ali in his prime.

The other part of taking the ocean for granted is I've fished for surfperch all my life. As a youngster, we made the 8-hour commute from northeastern Oregon to Neskowin every spring and summer. Dad drove around town hoping for a bargain-rate motel while we waited in the car (usually in the dark). If negotiations were favorable, he returned for Mom's blessing before sealing the deal. I rappelled wave-slick Proposal Rock to catch redtails that we gutted and scaled in the surf. Mom rolled them in flour and fried the soft, sweet meat on high to serve up a meal where we ate all we wanted.

Of course, this all happened before the days of bike helmets, child-restraint seats, and a pervert on every block. Back when large families were in vogue and you could afford to lose an occasional child off the back of your truck. Back when parents did not fear that their kids could end up as crab bait. Back when children ran loose to be entertained by nature, not electronic devices.

The day following Eric's sneaker wave incident was spent on my favorite rock point near Yachats. Looking out towards the western horizon, I wondered where the next crest would break. I counted waves and watched them swirl near my feet. I imagined swells building higher and higher. *They say every seventh wave is the highest; or is it every eighth? What kind of wave action tossed a two-foot-diameter log on the rocks and sent salt spray high enough in the air to leave crust on the plate glass window of our beachfront condo?*

My apprehension took a back seat, however, when a large school of redtails gathered over sand bottom where the river current met the sea. The bite-fest started with a distinctive sharp tick that I missed. *No big deal,* I thought. *I've got a two-hook rig. If I'm patient, another fish will find the other bait.* No sooner did I reel up slack than I experienced another bite. This time a hookset was achieved on a fish large enough to take out drag. I reeled up tight, timed a wave, and dragged two redtails onto the bedrock shelf at my feet. *I didn't miss the first bite after all. A double!*

Things progressed to a bite on nearly every cast. Thinking it was a good time to try artificial bait, I threaded a soft plastic Gulp Minnow on the top hook and a Pumpkin Grub on the other. Fifteen minutes without a bite ended that experiment. My next bait was bit before my 3-ounce pyramid sinker hit the sand, proving once again there is no substitute for fresh mussel.

Six large redtails soon languished in a seaweed-lined splash pool near my feet, attracting the attention of a small boy about 10 years old. "Can I have one?" he asked, after I nodded hello.

"Sure," I replied, thinking back to when I was his age. "Go ahead and pick one out."

He wandered off with the perch strung through its gills on a stick. Half an hour later he returned to admire my growing pile of fish. "Can I have another one?" he asked.

"What happened to the last one?"

"I lost it."

"Okay," I said, "but take a small one this time." When he reached for the largest one, I said, "No, not that one. If you can't take care of a fish that someone gives you, then you get a small one."

That's when he admitted he gave the first fish away to an angler further up the rocks. "Why did you do that?" I asked.

"He only had two fish."

Not that I mind having a small boy take advantage of my good nature, but my guess is he is either class president or in reform school by now.

I returned to the same rocky point at exactly the same tidal stage the next day but the nomadic school of redtails was gone. I watched offshore waves build offshore and gather near my feet while I cast without reward until my right shoulder was sore. Never in a hundred years would I have thought to experience a bite on every cast one day and nothing the next. I also admit to having a similar expectation for Eric's brief, yet harrowing, visit with King Neptune. Which only demonstrates that not all days on the water involve a clear path to logic.

Brothers Andy and Al Garcia jig for walleye in the upper Columbia River.

Part 3. Human Nature

Mystical experiences might not be transferable, but ordinary human behavior is knowable, given time and attention.

—Jim Harrison

one more LAST CAST

COULEE TOWN

CERTAIN THINGS TAKE PLACE on fishing trips that
need not be shared with your significant other. We're not talking shady drug deals, infidelity, or a night spent in the county
jail, but little things that, over time, add up in an incremental
way. Things you keep to yourself. Things you hope your buddies
don't spill their guts about. Things you don't brag about to your
grandchildren when Grandma is around. In my case, I have little
to hide except for a series of harmless events that happened in a
small town in northern Washington State.

It all started with my fascination of local patrons and an evening of pool in the Banks Lake Pub. In between my turn at the
stick, a steady string of people exited the back door only to return a few minutes later. Sometimes it was a single, sometimes
a twosome. Their in-and-out movement was like clockwork and
difficult to ignore.

I was occupied at the time in a game of nine-ball with a lis-
some blonde coed who held the attention of every red-blooded

male in the joint. Unfortunately, her skills surpassed mine and I was forced to give up the stick after losing two games in a row. That's when I decided to check things out. A diversion can be helpful when your moment in the limelight is over. The back swinging door led me to a large graveled courtyard enclosed on three sides by a 6-foot-high picket fence. A floodlight shone on a small group huddled around a bonfire. It was a gathering of smokers banned to the outside.

Being a sucker for sitting around a campfire on cool evenings, I went back inside to get Ken. He grabbed his beer and we joined to feed chunks of split pine to the fire while the same group of smokers came and went like the ebbing tide. It's funny how human nature works. Once people get comfortable with you, they open up. A simple nod of the head is often all it takes to prime the pump. People with opinion will talk your ear off. People with issues unload. Lonely people are only too happy to share their life story. I am reminded of the time I dressed up as a mime for a Halloween party. The fact that I did not utter a single word all evening failed to hamper conversation.

Sometime after a second round of smokes, Ken and I were deemed harmless, and two-way conversation about the weather was initiated. Half a pack of cigarettes later, they began to exchange personal information. A young couple described a series of recent real estate deals. A bearded man whose ponytail was carefully tucked under a greasy John Deere ball cap entertained about his latest brush with the law. A bespectacled redhead complained about her boss. When she learned we were walleye anglers, she shared a location where a friend fished. Without lighting up once, Ken and I had been inducted into the inner circle.

As the midnight hour approached and the crowd thinned, things got friendlier. A middle-aged brunette with droopy eyelids sidled over, pressed her chest against my arm and asked if I had any chocolate. Her teapot-shaped companion looked at her cell phone and said to Ken, "Darn, I was hoping to have phone sex but my battery just died."

Nonetheless, Ken and I made it back to the motel with a clear conscience.

Two years later, after another long day of jigging for complacent walleyes, I returned to the same pub to be greeted from the first barstool by a wild-eyed man dressed in fleece shorts and ragged T-shirt. "You're brave," I said, remarking on his scanty attire. "It was 25 degrees out there this morning."

He grinned and shared that he had burned the hair off his legs by standing too close to the outside fire pit. "Like a ruffed grouse," he said, flapping his arms and making a face like a bewildered bird. "I was just there doing the grouse thing, trying to stay warm. Look at me, I'm not really here."

I was impressed. "Do you do other birds?" I asked.

After a reflective pause, he pursed his lips and whistled a melodic string of notes. "That's a dipper bird," he said.

"My favorite bird," I replied.

"Mine too," he said, reverting back to the former grouse posture and posing in faux song mode before climbing back on the barstool.

These amusing adventures served as prelude to two occasions where my butt was grabbed. The first scene played out on a Friday evening at the Electric City Bar and Grill. A woman-only pool tournament was the main event and the bar was packed. My fishing buddies and I evaluated the situation before deciding to take over the shuffleboard table. We shoved pucks for an hour or so, and my patented left-hand slide was coming into form. Leaning over to make a play, with my back to the bar, I felt a strong grip on my right buttock. When I looked to my playing partner, he said, "It wasn't me." That's when I turned around to see a gray-haired woman in braided pigtails retreating to her barstool. "You stuck your butt out there," she said, as if to justify the action, and turned around to sip her beer.

Before I could make up my mind whether to be flattered or offended, a much younger woman came to my side and apologized. "Mom's had too much to drink."

"No problem," I said, but I kept my eye on "mom" for the rest of the evening.

As fate would have it, lightning struck again less than 100 yards up the road at the Banks Lake Pub. I had been amusing myself shoving handfuls of quarters in the jukebox when a middle-aged couple came in the side door. They were tall and slim and dressed in matching western-style outfits, complete with fringed leather jackets and black pointy-toed boots. We chatted about the weather and the general state of the economy. One thing for sure, it wasn't an intellectual exchange. When small talk waned, the man excused himself to get a couple of "tall Buds." That's when his female companion casually dropped the small leather coin purse she had been clutching. Being a gentleman, I bent over to pick it up. And that's when her right hand came out like the strike of a rattlesnake and grabbed my backside.

So much for letting the same dog bite you twice, I thought. Once again, passive denial came into play. When I handed over the purse, the woman gazed into the distance and whispered, "Thank you." It wasn't clear if the remark was intended as appreciation for the thrill of the grab or for my genteel manners.

There's only so much you should experience before introspection is required. I couldn't help wonder what I'd set myself up for. Was grabbing a stranger's hind end standard ploy among local female patrons? Did Coulee Town women brag to their friends over a cup of herbal tea, "I got another one!"? That I might have been perceived as easy did not come to mind.

Coulee Town isn't always about me. When you make the same trip with the same people to the same place for more than a decade, the list of interesting events tends to grow. There's the evening a belligerent Indian showed up spoiling for a fight and GM's negotiation skills were put to the test. The time Al sweet-talked the local hottie into a spin on the dance floor and reported copping a feel. Another trip involved two hookers who busted into a motel room where friends gathered (I wasn't present) and demanded they do business. We still haven't figured out who made that phone call.

Then there is time spent on the water. March weather is uncertain, to say the least. I've experienced days filled with sunshine, had the bottom of my boat filled with hail, and been blown off the water by 50-mph winds. Fishing can be equally unpredictable. I once caught four walleye on successive casts, but have also been the only angler to not catch a walleye in three days of hard fishing. Then there was the time I was accosted by a local walleye aficionado for keeping my largest walleye ever, an 8-pounder. "Why did you keep that fish?!" he yelled from the back end of the launch while we unloaded our catch from GM's boat. "You killed 10,000 eggs."

"Because he wants to eat it!" GM yelled back as I clambered down the riprap bank, fillet knife in hand. In other words, you never know what will happen.

But it's those Friday evenings at the local bar that makes the trips interesting. Time away from your cramped motel room, re-dundant FOX news, and revisits of the same old fishing story A chance to play shuffleboard, shove quarters into a jukebox, and experience local color. As for those inimitable evenings on the town, it seems that every professional sport has a collection of devout groupies: baseball, basketball, football, golf, soccer, NASCAR. Not to mention what actors and rock-and-roll artists have to put up with on a daily basis. But you wouldn't expect that a retiree-age walleye angler would have to fight off admirers in a neighborhood bar. The good news is, these harmless events led to only brief notoriety among fishing buddies. As a consequence, my status was not elevated to the point that culpability followed me home.

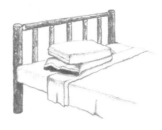

Two Pillow Sleepers

There's a fairly obscure country western song that goes like this: "I'm a two pillow sleeper. One catches the teardrops that fall. One right beside me to lie in your place."

Those lyrics played over and over in my head like a stuck record while I lay prone on a hard linoleum floor at the Westport Inn. Meanwhile, soft snores emanated from two nearby beds. Light from a neon flood lamp over the dock shone through a gap in the window curtains. My feet were wedged under a pot-metal television stand and my armpits were sticky with sweat. Cold air crept from a two-inch crack under the front door.

I would have been nestled like a mouse in a sock on a queen-size Beauty Rest except that Leroy changed his mind about sleeping in his van before Paul and I arrived. "Your friend has already checked in," the clerk said when Paul presented his confirmation sheet. Since Paul had paid for the room in advance and a rollaway bed was not available, I was relegated to either sleeping on the floor or shelling out for a separate room.

Okay. I admit it. I opted to put a 3-pound, poly-fill, child-size sleeping bag that was stashed under the backseat of my truck to good use. Sometimes you cheap out and get away with it and other times, "You get what you pay for," as my friend Bill often stated. I must mention that Bill grew up in a family that had money, and with money comes a different perspective on how to spend it.

Anyway, I set up in the narrow hallway of our shared motel room with a headrest that consisted of spare underwear balled up in a hooded sweatshirt. When it was time to turn out the lights, I asked Leroy if I could use his extra bed pillow to cushion my body.

"No. I need them both," he replied.

I knew that some people favored sleeping with more than one pillow, but was surprised when Leroy didn't oblige. First of all, he stole my bed. Second, he never used two pillows when we camped out on my boat. It was always that same, ratty old pillow with a brown knit cover that resembled a sweater your grandma gave you when you were eight years old. One you held onto like a snot-stained stuffed animal, until it fell apart. However, I also knew that once Leroy made up his mind, there was no use arguing, so I looked to Paul. Paul diverted his gaze and shook his head slowly from side to side. "I need both of mine, also," he said, as if it was all too obvious.

What the heck? Dang pillow hogs! Whatever. There was no point raising a stink, but I couldn't help wonder if the scenario was different, if we had selected a fine hotel with four pillows to a bed, if either Leroy or Paul would have found it in their heart to loan me one. But we weren't, and benevolence was not in the air. As a consequence, I spent a restless night on a cold, hard floor. Not to mention getting stepped on in the night when my pillow-hog companions visited the bathroom.

The Westport incident was all but forgotten until Ken and I traveled to Boggan's Oasis to fish for rainbows and smallies on the Grande Ronde River. Some downbeat experiences get pushed out of your head and some are buried, only to explode from your unconscious like the arm of Carrie from the grave. What happened next was an example of the latter.

The interior of our modest, pre-fabricated log cabin included a small refrigerator, microwave, kitchen table with two chairs, and a bathroom with shower. Two twin beds pushed against the wall and separated by the width of the front door completed the scene. Due to close proximity, I couldn't help notice when Ken grabbed a second pillow from the closet when it came time for us to retire for the night.

What the heck? Not another two-pillow guy! Whatever. Let's see how this plays out. "Miss the spousal unit already?" I said, hoping to obtain additional insight on the phenomenon of multiple headrests.

"I need one over my head," Ken replied.

"You mean to muffle your snoring?" I asked, remembering the last traveling companion who snored. After listening to the guy saw logs for an hour, I whacked him over the head with my pillow. I wasn't sure if Ken would respond favorably to some of the same.

"No. I've got earplugs for that," he said. "It's just the way I sleep."

I snuck a look in the night to see what made the second pillow so integral to Ken's sleeping habits. After my eyes adjusted to the dark, a swami appeared. Ken reclined on his side, the extra pillow wrapped around his head like a turban. *Whatever gets you through the night,* I thought. *At least you're quiet.*

The subject of two pillows didn't come up again until my sinuses began to drain down the back of my throat. Since I am a mouth breather, I was concerned about experiencing what I call a "choking dream." Nancy had the idea that I could avoid all that angst if I slept with my head elevated in a semi-reclined position. Like when you stretch out on the couch to watch TV. "Put the big pillow under the one you rest your head on," she said.

That would be two pillows, I thought. The result was eight hours of uninterrupted rest, although it wasn't clear if my visit from Mr. Sandman was due to the two-pillow arrangement or three-pill combination of Sinutab (decongestant), Benadryl (antihistamine), and Tylenol (pain relief) swallowed before I retired for the night.

Have I been missing something all these years? There is little doubt that a pillow is an essential element of your *boudoir*. Having the right amount of loft and "feel" can make the difference between a night of tossing and turning and restful sleep. Indeed, some people won't travel without their favorite drool-stained, head cushion whether stuffed with poly bead, horsehair, down, or cotton batting.

I've since given two pillows a fair amount of thought, although after researching the topic I found no mention of head wraps. What I did find was that stomach sleepers should place an extra pillow under their hips or ankles to take stress off the lower back and neck. Side sleepers, or individuals who choose to rest in a fetal position, might place a pillow under their head and neck to ensure their cervical spine remains straight and elongated. Placing an extra pillow between your knees helps open the hips. Two pillows can help alleviate snoring for back sleepers if one is placed under the head and another under the knees. Yet another choice is a body pillow, which provides an amicable "partner." None of these options, however, are viable reasons to make your fishing buddy sleep on a cold, hard floor while you dream the night away.

one more LAST CAST

A Fish for Mom

I've been bringing fish home to my mom like a tomcat de-livers dead mice to its owner since I was 12 years old. It goes back to the day I knocked a robin out of our sour cherry tree. I was first-string shortstop, had a good arm, and the dang bird was stealing fruit that could have been made into a pie. I'll never forget how Mom burst into tears when she saw what I had done. Needless to say, I buried the robin and have been trying to make up for the transgression ever since.

I like bringing Mom fish. It's easy penance. It was her silent smile of approval that sealed the deal for me to skip Sunday church service at age 16 and catch my first steelhead. Her love for break-fast fish helps justify keeping an occasional brace of rainbow trout. Shad are the only fish that don't bring a smile to her face.

Mom's modest three-bedroom bungalow is a short walk from the Walla Walla County fairgrounds. A step-across creek, rimmed with forget-me-not and baby orchids, borders her backyard. There's a shallow pond adjacent to the creek to harbor goldfish that attract great blue heron and the occasional urban raccoon. A family of mallards recently showed up. Papa drake proudly watched as 13 puffballs took a practice paddle. Assorted feeders populate a small flower garden as evidence of Mom's life-long passion for songbirds. It's nature in motion by the back door.

Following a recent successful trip for steelhead, I stopped by to process my catch on Mom's kitchen counter. She didn't have a fillet knife so I sawed the fish into a pair of small roasts using one of her serrated-blade steak knives. "These pieces can be wrapped in foil and baked in the oven," I said.

Two weeks later, I took the long way home after fishing the Tucannon River to deliver another steelhead. This time I came prepared with a fillet knife.

"How did those two roasts work for you?" I asked.

After a long pause, Mom replied, "I didn't eat them."

"The reason I asked is I thought I would cut this steelhead up into steaks. In case the portion size is better."

Mom remained tight-lipped until I bagged up the fish head and guts to bury under her rose bushes as Pilgrim fertilizer. "Actually, I gave one roast to Larry for helping me clean the pond," she said.

"That's okay by me," I replied. "Larry does a lot for you. He's a good neighbor."

Following another long pause, she added, "I gave the other piece to Tom. Molly's been sick."

"So you didn't eat any of it?"

"They really appreciated having it," Mom replied, "Although I was wishing I hadn't given it all away. That's why I was glad to see you with a fish."

"Confession is good for the soul, huh?"

About then a red squirrel launched off the back porch roof

and knocked loose a handful of sunflower seeds from a bird feeder. Mom banged on the sliding glass door and the squirrel raced to the other side of the creek to empty its cheeks.

Mom traps squirrels to get even with them for harassing her bird feeders. She is not so much bent on seeking revenge, as she loves birds. When you are 91 years old and your most reliable source of entertainment is watching wildlife out the kitchen window, you tend to get riled when an outside influence, such as a non-native species of squirrel, disrupts your daily ritual.

"It's not just about eating bird seed," Mom explained, "They destroy nests and eat baby birds." Mom battled squirrels at her collection of bird feeders for several years before resorting to live trapping. She euthanizes trapped squirrels by submersing the heavy-gage wire cage trap in her creek. "They don't feel a thing," she says. "I leave them in the creek for 10 minutes, drop them in a plastic bag and put them in the garbage can."

When I asked why she didn't take squirrels out of town and let them go, she replied, "They'll just come back."

"I got one!" she said the other day when I called to check on her. She didn't have to tell me what she got because I knew it was a pesky squirrel. "Is that the last one?" I asked.

"Nope. Two down, one to go," she replied. "A big one keeps tripping the door. I played with the mechanism, though, and think it will work next time."

In Mom's defense, she's not a cold-blooded killer. She has tried greasing poles that supported freestanding bird feeders, suspending feeders from cantilevered rafters and constructing elaborate climbing barriers, but squirrels eventually figured out how to get to her bird food. The last straw was an expensive "squirrel-proof" feeder that got emptied after one particularly clever squirrel figured out how to twist the top off.

Trapping squirrels has taken on a religious zeal between Mom and her closest friends. This fact became evident when I stopped by to deliver a breakfast trout. Mom wasn't home, so I put the fish in her refrigerator and left a note. As I walked out the front door, a car pulled into the driveway. A woman I did not recognize got out. Her sheepish look suggested she wasn't expecting to see me. "Can I help you?" I said.

"I'm Mary," she replied. "Is Priscilla home?"

"I think she's at the grocery store," I said. "I'm her son, Dennis."

Mary paused for several seconds before explaining, "I've got a squirrel in my trap in the trunk. Priscilla lets me drown them in her creek. It only takes a minute." She then elaborated as though reciting from the Good Book, "I'd let it go but it would just come back. They eat baby birds, you know."

On the way home I took a shortcut along the Walla Walla River via Frog Hollow Road, where I was reminded of fishing for steelhead with my friend Dick. Arriving back in the dark to where we started, I laid my hatchery steelhead in the snow, loaded my gear, and forgot about the fish. Until we got back to the Tri-Cities, that is. "There's only one explanation," I said to Dick, after we searched the back of my truck for the missing steelhead. "I left it by the side of the road."

The last thing I wanted to do was turn around and drive 50 miles back to the Walla Walla River, so rather than leave a perfectly good fish for a roving opossum to eat, I called Mom. "Would you drive five miles for a steelhead?" I asked.

She replied, "Sure. Where are you?"

"I'm home," I said, "but the steelhead is laying in a snowbank near the Boys Ranch. I can tell you exactly where if you will go get it."

Taking the request as if it was perfectly normal, Mom put Dad on the phone so I could provide directions. I gave them an hour before I called for an update. Dad picked up the phone to report that Mom backseat drove him the entire way. "Not sure it was worth the angst," he said, "but your mom was happy to get the fish."

The larger question was whether she ate the steelhead or used it for barter.

Leaky Waders

My bootfoot waders have been excommunicated to the back of my truck since they began to smell like oyster dressing. Admittedly, they have had a hard life. Battles with thorny brush, Rambo sticks and barbed wire first come to mind. The rear end is dirty, which requires pretending that others do not look there. Its roe-stained chest pocket is another badge of shame when in the company of fly fishers. As a result of constant exposure to "bait lint," the Velcro-lined flap no longer closes. Did I mention that the waders also leak? Believe me, there is a signal someplace.

Sooner or later though, all waders must be replaced. Hoping to find an off-season sale, I perused my pile of outdoor catalogs: Orvis, Cabalas, L.L. Bean, The Fly Shop, White River Fly Shop, The Fly Fishers Fly Shop, Bass Pro Shop, Filson, and Memphis Net & Twine. The sheer number and diversity of wading products was endless. All more high tech for sure than my first government-issue waders that came in only one size, extra-large, and one color, hatchery-worker black. The one feature that sticks in my mind, however, was a non-pliant crotch that hung down to your knees. A helping hand was required if you fell on the job.

But wading attire has gone to the next level. Retailers now feature multi-layer synthetic waders with welded seams. Some purport stretch and breathe fabric. Others showcase features that include articulated knees and abrasion-resistant legging. While reviewing catalogs, I was bewildered about the advantages of sliding H-back suspenders versus a three-point shoulder harness. Another consumer choice related to single front or paired side pockets. There was even a fleece-lined version that did double-duty as hand warmers. In other words, data overload.

Choice also had to be made between bootfoot or stockingfoot waders. If the latter, should I get accessory wading shoes with non-porous upper soles and closed-cell foam lining? I once owned a pair of rear-entry zippered wading boots that worked great until they shrank. That's where experience with snap-tie technology came in handy. One vendor went so far as to advertise ergonomic booties that matched the shape of each foot. Of course, anything innovative comes at a cost.

A related consideration in my search for bargain waders was whether to cater to the recently refuted allegation over transmission of water-borne disease via felt soles. Although several manufacturers offered "eco-friendly" solutions to safe wading, I was set on having felt traction soles with metal studs. You can survive only so many renditions of the funky chicken where fast current and slick rocks come into play.

More confusion reigned over a tapered waistline. Was this detail a fashion statement, or did drawstring waists stem the inward flow of water following an inevitable tumble? That question paled in comparison to the dilemma of whether to plunk down an extra $200 for a crotch-length watertight zipper. You could easily pay yourself a quarter every time you pulled down your suspenders and come out ahead on that deal.

A clear pattern emerged in my quest for dry feet: a thrifty attitude towards angling apparel in general. Consider the condition of lucky fishing shirts: missing buttons, torn sleeves, frayed collars, battery-acid holes. There's a cardboard box in the garage filled with old tennis shoes waiting to be recycled for summer wading. My favorite straw hat has a 6-inch gouge in the brim and my elderly steelhead vest is held together with clothesline cord. If a sock or a glove gets a hole in it, I save the good one, figuring to marry it up with another orphan later. Why do I keep worn-out crap? It's simple. I'm too cheap to shop for something new. Blame it on being raised frugal.

Back to my leaky waders. I wouldn't have pored through the entire stack of mail order catalogs except that water gushed from the left boot after my last fishing trip. And I don't recall wading past knee-deep. Only when I turned the waders inside out and inserted a trouble light down the leg was the source of the problem revealed: a series of minute tears in the fabric where duct tape failed to stem the tide.

Common sense aside, I plan to hold onto my leaky waders for winter walleye. Jigging for walleye involves standing in a boat with little risk of taking water over your big toe. Although impaired, my bootfoots provide ample protection against wind and rain. The next pair of waders, hopefully purchased on sale, will be hung upside down and shielded with cardboard to pro-tect from ultraviolet radiation. I've seen that done for RV and boat trailer tires. As for the ongoing challenge of roe stains and acquired odor, there's always a place in the back of the truck.

one more LAST CAST

A Spam Picnic

"Do you like Spam?" Dick asked.

Rather than respond straight out, I replied, "It's been awhile." A slight grimace may have been involved.

The brief exchange produced a flashback to the past, back to stay-at-home moms, low-budget meals and comfort food. In my childhood home, Spam provided a respite from inexpensive cuts of meat that included chicken liver and beef heart. It filled the protein gap between side dishes of macaroni, mashed potatoes, and steamed rice. Eating Spam on a regular basis was an experience in frugality I chose not to repeat with my offspring.

Still, with over eight billion cans sold since the meat product was unleashed on the general public in 1937, Spam couldn't be all that bad. Thinking back though, the last time I ate it was at a funky beachside restaurant in Hawaii. I had to go back another 30 years, to a backpack trip in the Wallowa Mountains with my son, Matt, for another example. On the last day of our 50-mile hike we fried up a can of Spam for breakfast. Being out of provisions, we followed that meal with a trailside lunch of Spam wedged between leftover pancakes.

Before I get too deep into the topic of sandwich fixings, I must mention that a bonus for going fishing with Dick is that he brings abundant food and drink. For Dick, fishing is merely an excuse to have a picnic. Nobody goes hungry. So when I told him I had to pack a lunch before we could launch the boat, he replied, "Don't worry. I'm bringing stuff to eat."

As it turned out, Dick brought two coolers for an afternoon of salmon fishing on the Hanford Reach. His son-in-law, Rob, joined us. One cooler was packed with assorted cold beverages and the other was full of food. After motoring upriver to Taylor Flats, I put their rods off the side holders and mine off the back. All three rods were rigged with a jet diver and sardine-wrapped Kwikfish.

There are days on the river when salmon come to your offering like sinners flock to communion. On this day I felt like the Messiah when my rod went down on the first drift and I reeled in a bright, 16-pound Chinook. A second drift through the same location yielded another takedown. This time I handed the rod to Rob. His fish tipped the scales at 20 pounds. "My first salmon on the Columbia," he said.

"It looks like they prefer old thumper," I said, in reference to the attractive erratic action of my K-16 Double Trouble Kwikfish. Thinking that size really does matter, I swapped out Dick's fire-engine-red K-14 for a chartreuse-splashed K-16 that quickly led to another salmon. "Maybe we should quit while we're ahead," I said.

"Are you kidding me?" Rob said. "I plan on staying until we get our limits."

That's when Dick pulled out a six-pack of Bud Light and a box of fried chicken. "From your favorite delicatessen?" I asked.

"Walmart," he replied, chewing on someone's idea of a chicken breast. (Not mine. The ratio of white meat to "back meat" was too high.) "Want some?"

"Sure," I said. "But I thought we were going to eat Spam."

"I'm saving that for later. After we catch another salmon."

Three hours and two more fish in the box later, the sun touched down on the desert horizon. Salmon rolled and jumped on the water's surface like a school of friendly dolphins. It was peak migration, and they were on the move to nearby spawning grounds. That's when Dick pulled out the Spam sandwiches. "I'll try half," I said, hoping to ease into my encounter with this mysterious Renaissance meat that now comes in 12 different varieties including teriyaki, jalapeno, oven-roasted chicken, and hickory smoke.

"You get a whole one," he said, handing me a ziplock plastic bag. "I brought two apiece."

The pressure was on. With a critical eye, I examined the contents. The sandwich consisted of a cold, thick slice of "shoulder of pork and ham" nestled innocently between two slices of white bread. "Did you add condiments?" I asked, in a weak attempt to stall.

"Only a smear of mayo," Dick replied.

I tried not to dwell on the meat's mottled appearance. *Exactly how much animal protein is involved in production? Is it an upgrade from bologna? Would it make good crab bait?* Not surprisingly, lyrics to the 1970 Monty Python classic played over and over in my head, "Spam, spam, spam, spam, spam . . ."

One thing was evident. Spam would not win a beauty contest when lined up next to deli-cut pastrami, roast beef, or Black Forest ham. I also remember thinking that a generous leaf of lettuce and a smear of gourmet mustard would have enhanced the experience.

My first bite into the sandwich could be characterized as tentative, a defensive move that captured as much bread crust as possible. Once the bolus ricocheted past my taste buds, however, I was pleasantly surprised to experience a bold, rich flavor coursing through my veins. The exotic six-ingredient "mashup" of pork, water, salt, potato starch, sugar, and sodium nitrate promised more, but in a guilty pleasure sort of way. An important question remained, though. Would you still respect yourself in the morning?

As things turned out, I didn't have to pay penance for gluttony nor risk gastronomic disorder. Midway into the fourth or fifth bite (I was not counting), a rod tip went down, and in the excitement, my Spam sandwich hit the deck. It wasn't until we netted our fifth salmon of the afternoon that I thought about the fate of my half-eaten repast. Not wishing to hurt Dick's feelings, I hid what now resembled a badly mangled roadkill in the jockey box of my boat.

I later noticed that Dick went straight for a handful of Pringles potato chips after he wolfed down his Spam sandwich. *To kill the taste?* I wondered, although I would have preferred to chase my sandwich with something stronger. Doritos Cool Ranch or Nacho Cheese chips, for example. Nonetheless, I had no complaints. Like my Grandpa Harry used to say, "Don't look a gift horse in the mouth."

The same goes for what your neighbor might bring along in a picnic basket or drink cooler. You are best served to take what is offered, especially on a warm, sunny afternoon when salmon are biting.

TRAIL OF EVIDENCE

THERE ARE THREE THINGS about fishing that frost wife Nancy's backside. First on her no-no list is evidence of egg cure on her new granite countertop. Second is finding fish scales in the sink. Third is someone stinking up the house with the smell of smoked fish.

As for the former, bait stains happen nearly every time I prepare a fresh batch of roe. It doesn't matter how many layers of newsprint I lay down. No matter how carefully I spread dry cure on the loose skein of a salmon or steelhead, the persistent pinkish stain of Pro-Cure or loose crystal of Borax shows up someplace in the kitchen. Bait cure acts like a virus that way, spreading from the source to places you can only imagine.

I don't consider myself messy, having been trained as a child to clean up after myself. It's just that I'm red-green colorblind. Not so bad that I can't tell a red light from a green light; rather, pastels confuse my cone cells. The result is that pinkish hues from bait cure tend to disappear from view where they compete with brown and gray. In other words, don't let me pick out your wallpaper.

Along with superior eyesight, Nancy's got an acute sense of smell that allows her to discern between single-malt Scottish and Irish whiskey. She's proven these olfactory powers with a single sniff while blindfolded. In contrast, my sense of smell is muted by years of exposure to paint fumes, sawdust, and formalin. I bring this up as partial explanation for why my latest attempt to smoke a batch of fish created a brief stir.

Three racks of mountain whitefish and steelhead were placed in the smoker from 9:00 a.m. to dusk as hors d'oeuvres for Thanksgiving dinner. Unfortunately, my Little Chief struggled due to air temperatures that dipped below freezing. It wasn't until I brought the fish inside that I sensed it wasn't quite done. Nobody I know likes to eat raw fish, so I put the batch in the kitchen oven to finish it off. You guessed it. The entire house smelled like smoked fish. I cracked the window, turned on the ceiling fan and ran the oven vent on high, but it didn't help. So much for an open-concept room design. The topic of odor control is not brought up on the Home Improvement channel.

Things settled down after the smell of roasted fish flesh dissipated and all was forgotten until Nancy woke up hungry for cinnamon toast. (Notice I didn't say *forgiven*.) My recipe for cinnamon toast involves the toaster. I spread copious amounts of butter on toasted bread and sprinkle on heaping tablespoons of white sugar and cinnamon. The result reminds of a *churro* or an elephant ear at the county fair. Nancy makes her cinnamon toast the old-fashioned way. She butters a slice of bread, sprinkles sugar and cinnamon on top, and broils the concoction in the oven until the surface takes on a metallic glaze. Unfortunately, she chose the same pizza pan to broil her toast that I used to finish off the partially smoked steelhead. The same pizza pan I put back in the kitchen cupboard after a half-assed job of scrubbing off baked-on fish skin.

You guessed it. Her cinnamon toast tasted like smoked salmon and I got reamed.

I must also mention that Nancy has a detective mind-set. You are guilty until proven innocent. She once got rejected from jury duty after telling the screening lawyer her favorite television show was *Perry Mason*.

"Where was the last place you saw it?" she asks when she catches me wandering around the house looking for a lost object. "You need to reconstruct what you were doing and where you went."

Nancy pulled up in the driveway recently to find me cleaning out my small boat cooler. The one I use for food and drinks (and bait, when I can get away with it). I had just returned from a pink salmon trip on the Skykomish River with the grandkids and the cooler was a mess. "What did you do, get too much fish slime on it?" she said. "Ha, ha. As if you care."

Admittedly, cleaning any cooler is a seminal event for me. "The grandkids spilled pop all over the inside," I replied. "Soda pop is sticky and attracts ants, if you must know." (Diversion is always my first line of defense.)

"Whatever. Why is the big cooler out?"

"I thought I would wash it while I was at it," I replied, hoping she wouldn't put two and two together and figure out that I had hauled salmon home in it. "It got dusty during the drive to the cabin last month." It ain't lying if there's a grain of truth in your story. It's merely elaborating.

As usual, Nancy was a half-step ahead of me. "You sure about that? You better not start using the good cooler for fish."

Good cooler? I thought. The lid lacks hinges but stays in place if you tie it down with a sash cord. It's dented on two sides and the inside has pink splotches where cured eggs once found a home. As if reading my mind, she tossed out, "I'll just buy a new one."

"We've got plenty for intended purpose," I replied, reflecting on the large collection of mismatched coolers scattered about the garage.

What saved my bacon on the fishy cooler was Nancy's previous directive not to bring a single salmon home. But what she didn't know was that Matt asked me to bring *his* share back to be smoked. She also had no knowledge of the 20 pounds of pink salmon I had already filleted and placed out of sight (and out of smell) in the freezer. That left loose fish scales in the kitchen sink as the only other trail of evidence to cover up before the Perry Mason side of her brain kicked in.

BUCKS AND DOES

My enlightenment on the vernacular of salmon gender can be traced back to when Bob bragged about a recent fishing trip on the Hanford Reach of the Columbia River. "Caught a big ol' red-sided buck yesterday," he said.

"How big was it?" I asked.

"A teener. Maybe 15 pounds."

When I first started to catch the occasional salmon, I referred to their gender as either male or female. Little did I suspect that conversation would get more complicated, that my piscatorial vocabulary would need to expand if I wanted to keep up with my fishing buddies around the water cooler. *Teener buck, huh?*

I knew mature Chinook salmon developed large, sharp jaw teeth during breeding. One purpose was display when fighting with other salmon over territory. I also knew that their upper jaw enlarged as they approached spawning time, eventually extending downward to form a hooked snout. These things I had seen firsthand. But having been raised a Podunk trout fisherman in the hinterlands of northeastern Oregon, that day was the first time I had heard someone refer to a male salmon as a "buck."

Upon further scrutiny, it turns out the term has merit. The Latin name for Pacific salmon, genus *Oncorhynchus*, is derived from Greek words that loosely translate to "hooked snout." As a consequence, the oddly shaped head and jaw of mature males lends some credence to the angler moniker.

There's more. It wasn't a week before my friend Geoff showed up with a fishing story of similar pedigree. "I caught a 20-pound hen yesterday evening," he said. "I knew it was a girly girl as soon as I felt it pecking on my Kwikfish."

Hen? Girly girl? Huh? "So how did you know it was a hen?" I asked, feigning knowledge of the gender connection while trying to get a handle on angler lingo.

"Bucks rarely peck at a lure," he explained.

Obviously I had more to learn about the nature of a strike.

Then there was a fall morning on the Yakima River when I overheard two guys talking. I wasn't snooping. Sound carries over water. "Got one, huh?" the first guy said.

"Yup. A nice one."

"Is it a buck or a hen?"

"I don't know. It's not very fat so I think it's a buck."

"You need to look at the anus."

Evidently, the vernacular of fish gender confuses, independent of which end of the fish you choose to examine.

It need not be so difficult. For example, since male salmon are called bucks, you would think that a female salmon would be called a doe. After all, it works that way for deer. I have seen the word *doe* used in the aquaculture industry to describe the female of a species, and the word also occasionally pops up in vintage sporting magazines such as *Outdoorsman* and *National*

Sportsman.

If only to reassure, I searched for the word "hen" in my deskside library. We're not talking Wikipedia-level research here. While nowhere to be found in the iconic reference *Henderson's Dictionary of Biological Terms*, Grandpa Harry's well-worn copy of *Webster's New International Dictionary* (the 3,000+ page, 10-pound, India paper edition) did not fail. I found that back in 1913, Noah Webster defined hen as both a "female bird" *and* "females of various aquatic animals," including lobsters or fish. If you think about it, the only thing these creatures have in common is that they all lay eggs. Accordingly, and given the general lack of logic for angler rhetoric, you might call a male salmon a rooster (or a cock, if you're from the UK). Just don't expect Webster to back you up.

To summarize this linguistic confusion for discriminate anglers and scholars of woodland lore—and at the risk of beating the topic to death—buck is the appropriate masculine version of deer and fish. It follows that hen describes the feminine side of birds, fish, and lobster. The terms *rooster* and *doe* are best reserved for specific genders of game birds and cud-chewing mammals, respectively. However you choose to embellish your fishing yarns with "teener" and "girly girl" is entirely up to you.

one more LAST CAST

SCENT AND SENSIBILITY

LEROY AND I WERE without a bump after several hours of mindless trolling that started well before sunrise. Meanwhile, I couldn't help but notice that other anglers had hooked up, their excited cries punctuating the morning stillness. What was our problem? We worked the same section of river, trolled the same speed and used the same gear. Was it the ol' stinky finger syndrome or what?

Maybe so. Out of the corner of my eye, I spotted a disheveled guide threading a cut-plug herring on a two-hook mooching rig. The only dressed-up part of his attire was a pair of bright-blue surgeon's gloves. The bend-over-and-grab-your-ankle kind your personal physician pulls on during the "back end" of your annual physical. After he builds trust by looking in your ears and nose for unusual objects and taps your knee to see if your leg responds with an involuntary kick. The same elastic blue gloves that guide his index and middle finger to your prostate. Teenage boys fear their first "turn your head and cough" exam. Mature males are equally nonplussed when subjected to the annual "finger wave." Both exams involve plastic "glovery."

When Leroy gave me a quizzical look, I was quick to remind him that plastic gloves are for the medical profession, food workers, and chemical handlers—not fishing partners. I had no choice but to lay it on the line. A glove craze has ramped up among anglers like flotsam carried in a tidal wave. And the practice of wearing gloves to prevent the transfer of human smell to your bait is not restricted to guides and tidy baiters. I've observed fly fishers casting for steelhead wearing stretchy hand protectors. As near as I can tell, the approach appears to be a generation thing. I don't recall ever seeing an old-timer put on gloves to thread a night crawler on his hook. "Like washing your feet with your socks on," my Uncle Chuck would have said.

Admittedly, the idea for eliminating repellent odor took root with sound science. For example, it's been demonstrated that fish can detect certain metal and organic compounds at concentrations as low as 10 parts per billion—a sense of smell that equates to a mere drop of water in a kitchen sink. It's also been shown that salmon avoid the odor of bear paws and the human hand dipped in water. These grains of truth apparently pack a wallop for some folks, with gloves being the principal "scent blocker" for anglers.

Scent protection can be taken to the extreme. Only recently, I pulled into a launch to find a guy hosing off the back of his boat. You guessed it. He sported blue plastic gloves. "I leave all the blood and slime on my boat," I said. "Otherwise, my buddies don't believe I catch any fish."

The angler gave me the stink eye. Okay, maybe he was trying to keep the odor of fish off his hands, a more practical application of plastic gloves. Still, some people have no sense of humor.

I thought of suggesting camouflage-color gloves to avoid looking like a roving proctologist, but he was bigger than me so I kept the thought to myself.

You know how sound carries over water? Well, I was walleye fishing up at Lake Rufus Woods once and overheard two guys conversing. One said to the other, "Ever light up a cigarette while you're putting on a worm and catch a fish on the next cast?"

The other guy wasted no time replying, "I recall doing that once. Worst case is you aren't deprived of a smoke."

So they both lit up. Neither wore hand protectors. You guessed it. They hoped to generate a nicotine bite.

Here's an idea. Rather than fuss with the impossible task of masking odor excreted from the sweat of your palms or transferred via spicy items in your lunch, why not add the odor of fish to the occasion? Consider the old adage, "It takes a criminal to catch a criminal." Maybe you have to smell like a fish to catch a fish. A related objective is not touching certain parts of your body when fishing, such as those in the orifice category.

Staying with that train of thought, it would be easy to expand the use of scent products like Smelly Jelly, Mike's Herring Oil, or Lunker Lotion along lines of personal hygiene. Bait scent could be applied like French perfume to touch up your ear lobes, neck, wrists, or any part of the body that stray fingers might touch during the course of fishing. Indeed, as a test of this "scent attraction" theory, I once worked up a green-label bait herring like a bar of soap and rubbed the greasy emulsion on the hands of a fish-less friend for good luck. Wouldn't you know? He was the recipient of the very next takedown.

The idea of masking your scent is not far afield. For example, hunters wear custom jackets, bibs impregnated with scent-blockers, and other clothing advertised as having properties that remove human scent. In theory, such odor-killing products mask the use of tobacco, allow for visits to the outhouse and encourage hemorrhoid scratching. A more practical approach for anglers would be to let your wife bait the hook. The odds are good that her brand of hand lotion is more attractive to fish than your 15-year-old aftershave.

On a personal level, I have a roe-stained sweatshirt that is soaked with the blood and slime of one hundred salmon and steelhead. To maintain its charm, I mop up the boat and cutting board with it after a day of fish carnage. Only recently was I forced to wash the sweatshirt. Something to do with being on the receiving end of bite marks from a small army of nits and fleas that took up residence while it resided in the backseat of my truck. As a consequence of being scrubbed clean, my lucky sweatshirt didn't catch fish for a month.

Which reminds that Nancy once had the gall to force a new sweatshirt on me. "It's time to get rid of that old fishing shirt," she said. "It's stinking up your new truck."

"But it's good luck."

"Too bad. I'm tossing it."

"You might as well toss me. We both have plenty of fish-catching left."

"We're talking about clothes here."

"Okay. I'll try the new sweatshirt. But it had better not put the skunk on me." (Translation: the old one will be kept hidden in the garage—a place she never goes—in case I need to retrieve it. After all, fish seem to appreciate its scent.)

LOSING IT?

"I'M IN THE MOOD for a fish dinner," Nancy said. "Why don't you pick out a nice piece of salmon?"

Before taking advantage of her suggestion, I inventoried and rearranged the upright freezer. I moved a package of Alaskan sockeye to the front, placed Chinook fillets planned as holiday gifts to the top shelf, and relegated steelhead two shelves down as a reminder to fire up the smoker. I ignored a year-old package of rockfish. There is no Goodwill for freezer-burned fish.

Settling on a shoulder fillet from an orange-meated spring Chinook, I was reminded of a guided trip to Drano Lake where, after reeling in a 17-pound springer at first light, I ended up with someone else's 13-pounder after the day's catch was divided at the launch. But that is another story.

On my way from the garage into the laundry room, I passed the upright rack that holds over a dozen casting and spinning outfits. Several more rods dangled from a rack mounted to the garage ceiling. A stack of gear bags leaned against a chest of drawers with extra reels, lures, and weights. The muddled scene reminded me that I'd recently donated several drift rigs to over-hanging brush on my last trip to the Tucannon River. *I need to tie up replacement yarn rigs. I could set up my vise on the dining room table, let the sun shine through the window, and listen to holiday music.* Holding onto that thought, I placed the package of frozen salmon on top of the clothes dryer and rummaged through the laundry room cupboard for colored yarn, bait hooks, and left-over spools of monofilament.

The next stop was at the hall closet to retrieve the c. 1960 fly-tying vise I use to tie up snelled hooks. I settled at the dining room table and organized my tackle. A pair of goldfinches hung off the thistle sock on the redbud tree. The odor of fresh-baked cinnamon rolls filled the air. There was a Christmas record play-ing, R&B as I recall, something about "Santa bring my baby back to me."

Soaking up the ambiance, I began to tie yarn drift rigs for steelhead: red, orange, chartreuse, blond, purple. You can never have too many color choices. I was still settled at the vise when Nancy returned from shopping an hour later. "Did you get the salmon out?" she said.

"Yup. And I rearranged the freezer to make it easier to find stuff."

"Where is the fish?"

"Thawing in the kitchen sink, unless a raccoon got it."

"It's not."

"I must have misplaced it," I replied. *Lost* is a four-letter word in my vocabulary.

I got up from the table and retraced my steps. Wouldn't you know? The fillet was right where I'd left it, on top of the dryer.

"Found it," I said.

"What would you do without me?" Nancy replied, rolling her eyes. "Tell you what; while you're on a hot streak, why don't you look for the Taj Mahal CD you lost two weeks ago, or the boat keys you lost sometime between yesterday evening and this morning?"

I ignored her banter. They say the mind tends to wander as you age, that you lose the ability to lock in on details like in your prime. I have no argument with that concept. Introduce me to a person, and their name will fly out of my head like bats fly from a belfry. I've got more acquaintances named "Hey" and "How're ya doing" than you can shake a stick at. I make detailed lists of things to do only to misplace the list. If my cholesterol meds didn't come in a sealed package imprinted with days of the week, I would lose track of dosage.

There's more. Items regularly make the transition from "misplaced" to "can't find" to "lost." Admittedly, these same items are not worth calling Search and Rescue or the Canadian Mounties over, but looking and not finding can take a toll on your mental state. There was a camping trip where I lost my wallet, only to find it in the bottom of my sleeping bag a day later. Was it waiting to be discovered, like Einstein's theory of relativity? What irked me the most was not the time wasted looking for it, but the three hours spent on the phone trying to get my credit cards turned back on.

On a recent trip to the Grande Ronde River, I left without my prized buffalo-hide fly satchel after searching without reward in all the usual places. I left my landing net hanging on a hook in the garage. I arrived on the river to find missing from my fly vest the soft canvas pouch that held over 20 Wooly Buggers. I forgot my kick fins and had to rely on wading sandals to navigate my pontoon boat through Class II rapids. Although these shortcomings were overcome, inconvenience comes to mind. You could say I was losing it, except that much of my life has played out this way.

Back to the dining room table. It was only after I'd tied a dozen steelhead drift rigs that I elected to look for the lost CD that Nancy mentioned. Two weeks is too long to go without listening to Taj Mahal's version of "Fishing Blues." The CD had to be in the truck, I figured, because I had systematically examined all 307 CD cases in my den and it didn't come up. I did, however, find several CDs I had forgotten about, in addition to some I couldn't remember buying. These observations were filed away for future reference.

Phase two of the missing CD search began by me opening the driver's side door of my Tundra truck and looking under the seat. The only visible item was a wrapping from a Hershey's Milk Chocolate with Almonds, a sight that triggered pleasant memories of a recent "buy two, get one free" experience at Safeway, where I ate one candy bar on the way home and stashed the other two for a future weak moment. *If only I could remember where I stashed the other two chocolate bars!* No sooner did I climb into the truck and look between the driver's seat and the center console than the glistening of a hard plastic case caught my eye. There, wedged in a narrow crack next to the floorboard, was a CD. My heart raced. *Taj Mahal has returned to the play list!*

One positive experience is often all it takes to get your hopes up for another. Holding onto that thought, I revisited the missing ignition key to my Hewescraft. Unfortunately, all I had to go on was a fading image of the key on the front edge of the master bedroom dresser and the knowledge it wasn't in a pocket of the zip-leg nylon pants I wore that day. I was also sure the key wasn't on top of the dresser with the rest of my keys because I had looked there twice. I tried to pin the loss on Nancy but she denied ever having it. Actually, she said, "Why are you asking me? You're the one who always loses things."

That left two plausible scenarios for the missing boat key. One strong candidate was "fell on the floor." A serious contender was "knocked into the dresser drawer." I'd already looked on the floor, but I got down on my hands and knees and looked under the bed in case I missed it the first time or someone kicked it along. According to the principal of strong inference, this fruitless outcome left "dresser drawer" as culpable. The top drawer held socks, pocketknives, and "important stuff" such as passport, memorial service programs and greeting cards. I had tossed all but two pairs of dress socks (one brown and one black) when I retired from the workplace, which left miscellaneous items and a wad of unsent greeting cards to rummage through.

The growing greeting card collection was a special challenge because, as Nancy is quick to remind, not everyone shares my sense of humor. One example was an experience that involved a Christmas card. Sometimes you buy things more for yourself than others, and this card was in that category. The front of the card had a colored illustration of Jesus. It was a familiar, pleasing image that reassured in a multi-denomination way. Three disciples were pictured in the background along with the words, "It's my birthday and I want a pony." I found the caption clever and only mildly irreverent, so I purchased it and added it to the card stack with no one particular in mind. Anyway, after sending off other cards to friends and family, the Jesus card remained. Rather than place it in the back of the card drawer, I thought of my ex-college roommate. A recent fishing trip on the Columbia River had rekindled our friendship, and led me to think he might be humored with the card.

Less than a week passed before the postman delivered a reciprocal Christmas card from Gary and his wife (his second wife, whom I had never met). I could tell Gary's new wife picked out the card because she signed both of their names. The front cover referred to God's blessings and the inside verse was from the Old Testament. *Uh oh, messed up that one.* Lesson learned: standard generic greeting cards will be sent to all non-family members next year.

Back to the missing boat key, which wasn't in the top dresser drawer under the thick wad of cards as predicted. Sometimes the second time through produces what you expected the first time, and other times it merely confirms your loss. I shifted my search to the second drawer down, the one that held my briefs and T-shirts. The messy drawer. Everyone's got a messy drawer to store junk in—whether it's in your garage, kitchen, or bedroom—and the second drawer in the large bureau I share with Nancy was mine. I couldn't help but reflect that its contents were packed tighter than a can of sardines. A neat freak would have dealt with the overload by rolling up individual items and assigning rows according to color or season of use. Another option would be to toss underwear that was stained, torn, or failed to conform to the body in an attractive manner. As a minimum, favorite briefs and tees could be segregated in separate, identifiable areas. Not me. That would be too much trouble. But I did have an organization scheme. All briefs were stuffed in the left side of the drawer (most recently washed ones in the back), while assorted short-sleeved tees filled the rest of available space. Some tees were rolled up to save space. Others were stuffed to save time.

Starting with the tees, I took a deep breath and began the extraction process, vowing to organize general categories of use after the search. This progressive thought was purged from my brain when the missing boat key appeared as if by magic under my Ray Troll "Fish Worship. Is it Wrong?" T-shirt. *How appropriate,* I thought, *I don't have to resort to secular prayer after all.* I stuffed the pile of loose tees back from where they came, strolled into the living room and announced, "Congratulations are in order. I solved two missing object mysteries in less than 30 minutes!"

"Good job," Nancy said. "What are you going to lose next?"

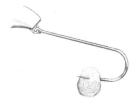

Everything Counts for Something

"Salmon are biting," BT said over the phone. "How would you like to pull plugs off Crab Creek?"

The idea of sitting on BT's boat on an Indian summer day was far more appealing than any other option I had pondered, most of which were destined to go unrealized due to incipient laziness. "Why not?" I replied. "It's my birthday and I can do what I want."

We anchored up in a current seam that paralleled a 40-foot depth contour, spooled sardine-wrapped Kwikfish off the back of the boat and watched our rod tips pulse in the current. Nary a breeze stirred the water's surface. A flock of Canada geese honked as they flew downriver. The hint of wood smoke hung in the air. Other than the steady report of bird cannons from a nearby orchard and the whine of semi-trucks down-shifting through Sentinel Gap, it was quiet. I couldn't help but feel that sometimes it's better to get cajoled into doing something rather than follow through on a half-baked idea of your own.

Back in those days, I was lucky to card one Chinook salmon a year. You could say I was a poor judge of success when it came to catching *Oncorhynchus tshawytscha*. By all accounts, however, salmon fishing was good. An occasional strike kept me alert, and we bonked two adults and a jack before mid-morning, or what my friend Greg refers to as "ham and egg time."

Then, sometime around noon, BT's cell phone rang. On the other end of the line was a buddy with a deep-seated need to live vicariously, and BT did not disappoint. "We've had an amazing morning of fishing," BT said. "Nine gnashes, six take-downs, five solid hookups, four salmon to the net and three fish in the box."

BT's conversation demonstrated that there is always something to be reported below the category of putting a fish in the box, that any and all rod action opens the door for casual elucidation. For example, anglers who drift shrimp under a steelhead float bobber are quick to report the number of "bumps," "take-downs," and "deep-sixes" they experience, in addition to the number of fish released or carded. Walleye anglers have several categories below a successful net job that include a "tick" (supposedly the result of a jig getting sucked past a sharp canine tooth), a "pull" (often confused with a weed) and a "head shake" (too embarrassing of a missed opportunity to admit, in my opinion). Fly fishers have a similar language. Don't think they don't. I've heard fly caster pals allude to steelhead takes as "pickups," "tugs," and "grabs." All of which are easily confused with the slide of your fly across the top of a boulder or the fin of a sucker. Not to mention the well-known "volitional release," a designation that describes a fish that pulls free before it can be slid to shore.

This dialogue leads to a story of a high school pal whose main claim to fame was copping an occasional feel with his elbow. In Willie's book of youthful tricks, rubbing up against any part of the female anatomy counted for something. A concerned friend once suggested he see a therapist. "They have a term for your behavior," she said. "You could end up on a neighborhood watch list."

Whether due to aberrant genes or a product of their environment, it seems that there's a Willie in every crowd. Consider a recent fishing trip. A group of us sipped brews in a crowded bar, discussed the subtlety of unrealized walleye bites and listened to the brand of loud rock music played only in remote corners of Washington State on Friday nights. In the midst of all the drinking and yammering, a friend I choose not to name calmly leaned back as if to ease his tired casting muscles. A subtle move, but we had seen it before. It seemed he noticed a buxom waitress approaching our table with no other option but to make herself small in order to squeeze past. My friend's timing could not have been more perfect. He "scored" with the backside of his elbow, and the waitress tipped his ball cap as if she had seen it all.

The point is that several tiers below closing the deal count in some people's minds, that in mannish sporting events involving your libido, elaboration on the general theme can be realized with the addition of a few well-placed adjectives or action verbs. Otherwise, life would be boring.

Anyway, I thought I had heard it all until BT and I were at it again. This time we fished for springers downstream of Ice Harbor Dam. We had been on anchor since dawn, but action had been limited to two brief hookups. I rationalized that springers are the best eating salmon on the planet because they are difficult to catch. If you can't dial up patience, then you should find something else to do. Like, mow the lawn, vacuum the living room rug, or hose spider webs off your back porch. Our patience was finally rewarded with an 11-pound hatchery buck that ran circles around the boat before I managed to get the net under it. The outcome left me yet to affirm my manhood.

Salmon fishing can be tedious in areas with mandated re-lease of wild fish (or non-clipped, since an intact adipose fin does not always equate to wild). Rather than all or nothing, your day might lead to something that counts for nothing, particular-ly if the objective is to bring home a fish dinner. Drinking coffee and eating snacks help fill empty moments, as does reminiscing about past conquests (including those that involve the opposite sex). Adjusting your drag, spooling out line, and swapping lures are my favorite displacement activities.

I'd worked through all three scenarios at least twice before I reeled in my Fickle Pickle 5.0 Mag Lip to refresh the sardine wrap with bait scent. Mike's Sardine paste, as I recall. The prod-uct comes in a 4-ounce white plastic container with red-and-yellow lettering and is dark-brown and thick, like the gravy your mom made from hamburger grease back in the days when moms made gravy. Before graphite rods, GMOs, and bikini-clad baris-tas. Back when your daydreams involved large fish and scantily clad women in equal proportion.

But I digress. Holding the Mag Lip up to the bright sky for contrast, I squinted to make sure the barbs were pinched down. That's when I noticed the faint glisten of a fish scale on a trailing siwash hook. "Check this out," I said to BT, positioning the tiny translucent scale on the tip of my thumb. "I've looked at enough fish scales to know this one isn't from a sucker."

"Wow!" he replied, "you scraped a springer. I don't know whether to count it or not."

I spooled my wrapped Kwikfish out with renewed confi-dence and forgot about the scale-scraping incident until BT's cell phone rang and he tallied the day's results to the friend having a deep-seated need to live vicariously.

"We are one out of three with a drive-by," BT said.

That's why, in matters that relate to fishing (or in Willie's world), everything counts for something.

one more LAST CAST